Guardian Angels

Discovering How to Connect with Spirit Guides, Angels, Departed Loved Ones, Archangels, Spirit Animals, Ancestors, and Other Helpers

© Copyright 2023 - All rights reserved.

The contents of this book may not be reproduced, duplicated, or transmitted without direct written permission from the author.

Under no circumstances will any legal responsibility or blame be held against the publisher for any reparation, damages, or monetary loss due to the information herein, either directly or indirectly.

Legal Notice:

This book is copyright protected. This is only for personal use. You cannot amend, distribute, sell, use, quote or paraphrase any part or the content within this book without the consent of the author.

Disclaimer Notice:

Please note the information contained within this document is for educational and entertainment purposes only. Every attempt has been made to provide accurate, up-to-date, and reliable, complete information. No warranties of any kind are expressed or implied. Readers acknowledge that the author is not engaging in the rendering of legal, financial, medical, or professional advice. The content of this book has been derived from various sources. Please consult a licensed professional before attempting any techniques outlined in this book.

By reading this document, the reader agrees that under no circumstances is the author responsible for any losses, direct or indirect, which are incurred as a result of the use of the information contained within this document, including, but not limited to, —errors, omissions, or inaccuracies.

Your Free Gift
(only available for a limited time)

Thanks for getting this book! If you want to learn more about various spirituality topics, then join Mari Silva's community and get a free guided meditation MP3 for awakening your third eye. This guided meditation mp3 is designed to open and strengthen ones third eye so you can experience a higher state of consciousness. Simply visit the link below the image to get started.

https://spiritualityspot.com/meditation

Table of Contents

INTRODUCTION 1
CHAPTER ONE: WHAT ARE GUARDIAN ANGELS? 3
CHAPTER TWO: TAPPING INTO YOUR HIGHER SELF 10
CHAPTER THREE: COMMUNICATING WITH YOUR GUARDIAN ANGEL 23
CHAPTER FOUR: WORKING WITH THE ARCHANGELS 36
CHAPTER FIVE: FINDING YOUR SPIRIT GUIDE 48
CHAPTER SIX: FOLLOWING YOUR ANIMAL GUIDE 57
CHAPTER SEVEN: CALLING UPON ANCESTORS AND DEPARTED LOVED ONES 65
CHAPTER EIGHT: CONNECTING WITH ASCENDED MASTERS 72
CHAPTER NINE: WORKING WITH GODS AND GODDESSES 81
CONCLUSION 88
HERE'S ANOTHER BOOK BY MARI SILVA THAT YOU MIGHT LIKE 90
YOUR FREE GIFT (ONLY AVAILABLE FOR A LIMITED TIME) 91
REFERENCES 92

Introduction

Guardian angels are waiting for you to find them. They are standing by to hear you call to them and to respond instantly. The reason why they are not responding is because you are not calling. And you are not calling because you are unaware of their presence. This book aims to dispel the darkness of unawareness and bring you the light of knowledge and acceptance.

Written in easy-to-understand languages and filled with detailed and easy-to-follow instructions and hands-on methods, this book on guardian angels is great for beginners taking shaky steps toward their goal. This book will help you firm up the shakiness brought on by initial doubts that prevent you from moving forward. It supports you until you find steady feet on strong ground so you can move forward to higher planes of consciousness.

This book covers all kinds of guardian angels who can come to your aid, from those who can protect you from harm, keep obstacles at bay, and give you materialistic benefits right up to those who can help you with ascension and enlightenment. This book covers a comprehensive list of guardian angels and instructions on reaching out to them and seeking their help and counsel.

For example, if you need protection, call out to Archangel Michael. If you seek wealth and prosperity, seek Goddess Lakshmi, and so forth. The book is not religious in any way. It is spiritual, dipping into all cultures and religions and taking the best each offers you. You will find connections between guardian angels, colors, symbols, and much more.

Every chapter in this book is filled with angel-seeking and soothing words of knowledge and light. You will be guided to open your heart, mind, and soul to receive the abundance your guardian angels are waiting to shower on you and your loved ones. Read slowly, savoring every word, soaking in the beauty of guardian angels and their powers, and knowing that the lessons taught in this book can help you feel the presence of the angels in your life.

A word of caution before you begin reading the book. Please note that the instructions given in this book are not intended to replace professional medical advice in any way whatsoever. Before trying out any practical exercises mentioned in this book, including meditation, rituals, and other exercises, please speak to a qualified medical practitioner and/or psychiatrist and let them know you are doing this. They will guide you in case of contraindications.

Go on, turn the page, read – and to remind you once again – read *slowly*, savoring every word this book contains, leading you to your guardian angels.

Chapter One: What Are Guardian Angels?

The concept of guardian angels and helper spirits is found in nearly all spiritual belief systems and religions of the world. These guardian angels are supernatural beings assigned by the divine world for the welfare of human beings on Earth. They are found everywhere.

St. Augustine speaks of guardian angels and angels as follows,

"Angels are spirits created by God. However, if they are simply spirits, they are not angels. If they are sent to do His bidding, the spirits become angels. God makes spirits angels by commanding them to do his bidding or order."

References to guardian angels can be found in the Bible.
https://unsplash.com/photos/DRgrzQQsJDA?utm_source=unsplash&utm_medium=referral&utm_content=creditShareLink

Many ancient texts, including the Old Testament, reference to guardian angels. Every religion has its own version of guardian angels. Let's look at a few.

Guardian Angels in Christianity

One of the first references to angels happens immediately after the fall of man (when Adam ate the forbidden fruit). A biblical verse goes like this, *"He drove the man out of His garden. He then placed the cherub along with a flaming sword to guard the tree of life."* Although the word "angel" is not used here, the definition of angel explained above makes the cherub one of them. God commanded the cherub to guard the Tree of Life. So, the first angel was created not for human beings but against them so they could not enter the Garden of Eden without His approval.

Another reference to angels comes when God sends "messengers" to warn Lot and his family about the impending destruction of Sodom. When Lot refused to leave, the "messengers" forced him out of the city, thus saving him, as commanded by God.

In the Gospels, Jesus calls his followers to respect every small and humble being in deference to the creature's guardian angel appointed by God to watch over it. God works His miracles through His guardian angels, protecting and providing for every form of life on Earth.

In Christianity, every person is assigned a guardian angel who stays with them right from the time of their birth until their death. Multiple saints and men of God from ancient and medieval times maintained the existence of guardian angels who live within His grace. These men of the church, like Saint Augustine and Tertullian, Saint Jerome, Saint John Chrysostom, and others, encouraged Christians to connect with their guardian angels.

Further, from the 17th century, the popularity of guardian angels increased considerably in the realm of Christianity, and Pope Paul V introduced the Festival of Guardian Angels to the Christian calendar. These angels found representation in all sacred events and among popular devotion and faith images. These angels were depicted as protectors, protecting everyone, especially children, from harm. Some pertinent points about guardian angels in Christianity follow.

The presence and existence of guardian angels are affirmed by the Gospels and Scriptures, supported by numerous examples and stories. The Catechism teaches followers to feel the presence of their guardian angels from their childhood and trust them.

Angels were created in thousands by the Divine Will in a single moment. After that moment, He did not manifest any more angels, and since then, the original angels have existed for eternity.

A structural hierarchy exists among the angels, and conditions must be met before becoming a *guardian angel*. The position and function of each angel are different, and not all of them are destined to become guardian angels. Some are called upon to take a test, and if they pass, they become guardian angels.

A guardian angel is assigned to every newborn child to remain with the person through their human life until death and beyond.

Every Christian has one and only one guardian angel who cannot be given away, shared, or sold. The primary function of this guardian angel is to guide people. He cannot interfere with their free will, cannot decide for them, and cannot impose choices on them. Those are theirs to make.

But your guardian angel is always by your side, trying his best to suggest a good way of life, avoid pitfalls, show you the right path, and light up your path to heaven. Christians believe that their guardian angel, most of all, helps them to be good people and faithful Christians. Guardian angels never abandon you, come what may.

Guardian Angels in Judaism

In the Old Testament, God is described as sitting in His heavenly court surrounded by spiritual beings who worship Him and do His bidding on Earth. All their actions are of, by, and through Him. The Hebrew word for angel is "malach" or "messenger."

According to Judaism, at every mitzvah (good deed or religious commandment/precept), angels are created who protect and shield followers from harm. Sometimes, God sends an angel as an emissary to help or guide you. After your death, these angels (created through belief work) testify for you in His heavenly court. It is important to remember that Judaism holds that an angel only acts as His emissary, nothing more and nothing less.

The four archangels, namely Michael, Gabriel, Uriel, and Raphael, find abundant references in Judaism. The archangels will be discussed in detail later on in the chapter. While only these four archangels find a hallowed place in ancient scriptures, many more angels appear in later antiquity. It was an angel who stopped Abraham from sacrificing his son. Another angel wrestled Jacob, and an angel of death too.

The Jews believe angels are subordinate beings and act in alignment with God's will. There are many other angel connections in Jewish liturgy, including:

- The famous Kedushah Prayer is believed to have been written from prophetic visions in which angels sang these verses.
- Wearing white on Yom Kippur reflects the belief that on that day of fasting and repentance, the Jews are like angels who rise above bodily needs.

Guardian Angels in Islam

Followers of Islam start their prayers with the acknowledgment of guardian angels, although no prayers are dedicated to them. Muslims recite Hadith and Quran verses that speak of guardian angels.

The quintessential Islamic greeting "Assalamu alaikum" translates to "Peace be upon you." Muslims say this phrase often by looking at their left and right shoulders because they believe that guardian angels referred to as "Kiraman Katibin," reside there. They believe it is appropriate and correct to acknowledge their presence in your life and are therefore included in their daily rituals.

This belief in guardian angels is rooted in various verses in the Quran, such as the following:

"Behold the two guardian angels assigned to learn every man's doings and actions, residing on his left and right side. Not a single word or act is left unnoticed by these appointed sentinels who are ever ready to take note of everything the man does or says."

The "Kiraman Katibin" angelic team works together to record every detail of the man's life to whom God has assigned them. The recordings are very detailed and include every feeling, thought, action, and word. The guardian angel on the right shoulder records the morally good aspects of the man, while the angel on the left shoulder records his bad choices and wrongdoings.

When the world ends, the " Kiraman Katibin" guardian angels will present the records of every human being they have worked with right through the history of humankind. God will send the men and women to heaven or hell, depending on the records of the guardian angels.

Another Quranic verse about guardian angels goes like this,

"For every person in this world, there are guardian angels going before and after him, protecting and guarding the man according to Allah's command."

Therefore, according to Islam, there are guardian angels for protection, too.

Hadiths (prophetic traditions written by Islamic scholars) also reference guardian angels. One such hadith by the scholar Muhammad al-Bukhari goes like this,

"Angels take turns around you. Some of them come by night, and some by day. All of them assemble during the Fajr (pre-dawn) and Asr (pre-evening) prayers. At night, they ascend heavenwards to meet Allah, who asks (even though He knows more), 'How have you left my beloved servants?' They answer, 'Just as we found them. Praying!'"

This hadith carries the message of the importance of prayer and the significance of guardian angels, both of which, according to Islam, help followers get closer to God. Guardian angels protect and pray for their assigned people and deliver messages to God.

Who Are Archangels?

There is also a hierarchical structure among angels, and archangels are at the top of the ladder. They are high-ranking angels created by the Divine Will to offer wisdom to human beings so that we can deepen our connection with Him and the universe He created. There are seven archangels referenced in various scriptures. These seven are Michael, Raphael, Gabriel, Jophiel, Ariel, Azrael, and Chamuel.

Every archangel has a specific role to play in the grand scheme of the cosmos, and each of their names also has a different and specific meaning and significance. Let's look at the seven archangels a little more in detail.

Michael - His name means *"He who is as God."* Aligned with warrior-like attitudes such as bravery, justice, and strength, Michael is here to protect humans. Michael is the most powerful and well-known archangel. He is the angel you call for help in moments of crisis. His wise guidance will help and protect you in your weakest moments. He is often depicted as a glimmer of blue light.

Raphael - His name translates to *"God heals,"* and as his name suggests, he is responsible for healing physical and emotional issues and ailments. Doctors and other medical practitioners seek Raphael's help whenever they need assistance. You can call him when you or someone you know is sick and needs healing which can come in the form of a miracle or a solution to restore the affected person's well-being. Raphael is depicted as a glimmer of green light.

Gabriel - Gabriel means *"God is my strength."* He is the angel of communication and the messenger of God. People working in the field of communication consider Gabriel their patron, although he excels at helping teachers, artists, and writers too. If you have trouble expressing or communicating your thoughts and feelings, seek Archangel Gabriel's help. He is associated with the color white.

Jophiel - His name translates to *"beauty of God."* His primary function is to make you see the beauty in God's creation and to redirect your perception to God's love in all that you see. Jophiel is the one you should call when you are stuck in a rut of negativity. He can guide you, shift your perspective, and redirect your life toward love. His color is yellow. Yellow should remind you that you need to change your perspective to find what you seek.

Ariel - Ariel means "Lion of God," and his job is to protect the Earth, her resources, and the life forms that inhabit Earth. He is the patron of environmental activists, animal lovers, and all things associated with Mother Earth and her resources. He is associated with the color purple.

Azrael - His name means "*whom God helps.*" Azrael's main role is to help the suffering and the diseases transition smoothly into the spiritual realm, and for this reason, he is also known as the Angel of Death. If you are facing a lot of losses and deaths, call Archangel Azrael to ease the pain and reduce the losses. However, "death" need not be taken in the literal sense. Job changes, moving home, doing things in a new way by discarding the old, starting a new relationship, etc., are also situations where Azrael can help. Azrael's color is indigo.

Chamuel - Chamuel translates to *"he who sees God."* His responsibility is to bring peace to the world. He is created with the power to bring order even in the most chaotic situations. If drama and conflict surround you, call upon Archangel Chamuel to restore peace and harmony. He is associated with the color pink.

Four of these seven archangels have more importance than the other three, which will be discussed in a later chapter dedicated to archangels.

In summary, regardless of the religion, guardian angels are spiritual beings and higher-order angels assigned to each person by the divine to help them through their lives. Most importantly, for all people seeking help from all corners of the cosmos, guardian angels come in many forms. They could be tangible in the form of other wiser and more experienced humans. Or they could be a product of your subconscious mind as you seek a respite from life's burdens and challenges.

Regardless of their form and regardless of which religion or belief system you follow, what matters the most is the keenness or your desire to resonate with them and find ways to reach out and take what they have to offer. And even more important is to be open to having experiences related to guardian angels. It could be an unreasonable expectation if you lock your heart and mind and expect supernatural beings to knock on your door. Keep your heart and mind open to the magic of guardian angels, and you will be able to harvest the advantages of these wonderful beings.

Chapter Two: Tapping into Your Higher Self

Communicating with the invisible, spiritual realms requires you to be prepared with theoretical knowledge *and practice*. You need to know where and how you can access these realms. You need to know the elements that can help you tap into your higher self, one that is usually dormant until you make an effort to awaken it. Four of the most important elements that help you access the invisible realm are the spiritual body, the higher self, the chakra system, and the aura body. Let's look at these three individually and understand how they work.

The chakra system can help you connect with the invisible realm.
https://pixabay.com/images/id-5628622/

The Spiritual Body

Jill Willard - a powerful Intuitive and a leader in the practice of meditation - says that the human body is composed of four distinct parts: the physical, emotional, mental, and emotional. Three of these four parts are seemingly tangible, but each body contributes 25% to your wholeness. Your body's physical, emotional, and mental aspects are clear, and most people know them and have experienced them and their effects on their lives. Thus, it's worth discussing the spiritual body.

So, what is the spiritual body? It is that which connects you to all the things in this cosmos, including the Earth and beyond, God (or the Divine Will), and your higher self. The spiritual body protects and guides you from a source outside and beyond the five-sense world you know and experience daily. The spiritual body connects you to everything in this external source, spirits, angels, divine beings, and everything outside the physical realm.

Many people are unaware of the existence of the spiritual body, a facet of life that has nothing to do with the religion you follow or the culture to which you belong. The spiritual body is an element that tells you that no one in this world is alone. Everyone is interconnected, and it takes more than just one physical body and its mental and emotional aspects to create and sustain life in the universe.

When your spiritual body is balanced, you feel calm and fearless and can work without anything limiting you. You get the fortitude and support to concretize your ideas in the physical realm. You know for certain that there are realms that are way beyond what the average human being can access. With repeated practice of knowing and understanding your spiritual body, you can access the invisible realm where guardian angels reside.

The Higher Self

In most spiritual discussions and talks, you come across words like, "Connect with your highest self to achieve peace, calm, and self-actualize." But what is this higher self? Can it be described? And how can it help you to achieve all that it promises?

The higher self is that part of you that goes beyond your physical body. It inspires, guides, and teaches you through your instincts and insights. Your higher self is well aware of your secret dreams and goals.

However, most people do not really try to connect with this part of themselves because, first, many are unaware of its existence, and those who know it either doubt it or find it difficult and tricky to connect with it.

In the language of psychology, the higher self is an inner guidance connected with the cosmos and separate from your physical, emotional, and mental personality. It is also not your ego, even though it can advise you about your ego. The higher self connects the material world to the mystical, invisible world. Your higher self is part of you, although it operates at a higher vibrational frequency than your physical body.

Your physical body is the current human life that you are living, whereas the higher self is the spiritual component that has seen and lived multiple lives. A life without any connection to the higher self is limited to the physical realms. Such lives are easily swayed by the temporary, feeble aspects of the physical world that lack authentic, sustaining inner strength and power. When you connect with your higher self, you get multiple benefits, including:

- Regardless of what is happening in your physical life, you feel fulfilled, and your life feels magical.
- Your life events are more purposeful, and you don't resent any of the experiences you face.
- You know and accept that pain is not an obstacle but an opportunity for growth and development.
- You feel supported, connected, and empowered.

The Chakra System

Chakra is a Sanskrit word meaning "*disk*" or "*wheel.*" According to the ancient Indian Yoga system, chakras or wheels of energy reside in strategic places aligned with the spine. These wheels of energy cannot be seen but felt, and their power can be invoked to connect with the invisible realm. The healing energy in these chakras forms your body's vital life force, which keeps the body active, strong, healthy, and powerful.

The chakras hold the energy of your feelings, thoughts, past memories, experiences, and future insights. How do these chakras help your well-being and your ability to connect with your guardian angels?

First, your body, mind, and spirit are all interconnected. Therefore, an imbalance in any of these three aspects will impact your entire being. You may have heard of many cases where physicians could not find a physiological reason for someone's illness, yet that disease existed in the body. In such cases, the root cause could be something in the mind or spirit. For example, a woman who has lost her beloved husband can get acute stomach pain or heartburn that may never have a physiological cause. Her physical ailment is rooted in the grief of her broken mind and spirit that she has yet to overcome.

There are seven main chakras, the first at the base of the spine and the last on the crown of the head. Each chakra is associated with different parts of your physical, mental, emotional, and spiritual body. The chakras have to be balanced and energy flow in them unblocked for optimal benefits. Let's briefly look at each of these seven vortexes of power and energy and how they help you to maintain your equilibrium.

The root chakra: Located at the base of the spine, the root chakra (or the Muladhara in Sanskrit) is connected to your basic survival needs, such as food, sleep, shelter, and other basic materialistic needs. When this root is unbalanced and/or the energy flow is blocked, you experience existential fears, and when balanced, you feel safe, secure, and stable.

The sacral chakra: Located two inches below the navel, this energy vortex (Svadhishthana in Sanskrit) is responsible for the reproductive organs, including the testes and the ovaries. Your sexual energy is stored here, and therefore, it is connected with all your relationships. When the sacral chakra is out of balance, you tend to overindulge or under indulge in your sexual endeavors. When the energy flow is unblocked, you tend to have harmonious, happy relationships.

The navel chakra: Located at the navel, this chakra (Manipura in Sanskrit) is the seat of the digestive fire and deals with the functions of the adrenal glands and the pancreas. A person with an unbalanced navel chakra tends to be overly domineering or completely powerless. A balanced navel chakra is a source of enthusiasm leading to empowerment and the ability to achieve your goals. The navel chakra is also called the solar plexus.

The above three chakras represent the physical realms. The four chakras discussed below are associated with the mental and spiritual realms.

The heart chakra: Located in the center of the chest, the heart chakra (Anahata in Sanskrit) is associated with love and connection. It also bridges the upper spiritual chakras and the lower physical energy vortexes. An unbalanced heart chakra manifests in the form of excessive possessiveness and/or an unreasonable desire for constant attention. A balanced heart chakra translates to the start of experiencing an expanded consciousness.

The throat chakra: Located at the center of the throat, this energy vortex (Vishuddha in Sanskrit) is associated with communication and expression, specifically with that of truth and authenticity. When this chakra is blocked, you tend to have difficulty communicating and expressing yourself. This chakra is an excellent source to connect with our authenticity and purity when opened and balanced.

The third eye chakra: Located between the eyebrows, this chakra (Agnya in Sanskrit) is the seat of the mind and the center of your intuition. A blocked or unbalanced third eye chakra prevents you from connecting with your higher self, while a balanced, free-flowing status allows you to control your mind and, through it, your body.

The crown chakra: Located at the top of your head, the crown chakra (Sahasrara in Sanskrit) is the center of enlightenment and the bridge connecting you to your higher self. It is the seat of your soul.

Importantly, the chakras' alignment must be taken step-by-step and gradually. It is impossible to awaken or unblock the Sahasrara without caring for the lower chakras. You have to start with the lower chakras, get your physical body in order, and then move up to the higher energy vortexes until you reach the crown chakra, which, when opened, will give you limitless access to the invisible realm, the seat of divine beings including your guardian angels.

The Aura

Every living thing in this world has an aura, the invisible spiritual field surrounding the body. There are seven layers in this aura body, each of which relates to different elements of your physical, mental, emotional, and spiritual health. The seven colors of the aura body and their connotations are as follows:

- **Red** - The red aural layer represents being energetic, well-grounded, and having a strong will.

- **Orange** - Orange aura stands for being adventurous, considerate, and thoughtful.
- **Yellow** - Stands for being friendly, creative, and relaxed.
- **Green** - Stands for being nurturing, having good social skills, and communication.
- **Blue** - Stands for freethinking, being a spiritual seeker, and being intuitive.
- **Indigo** - Represents being gentle, curious, and spiritually connected.
- **Violet** - Stands for independence, wisdom, and intellect.

The intensity of the colors of these seven layers describes the depth and complexity of the various traits. Your higher self can be felt, experienced, and even seen in your aura, and it appears like a radiant point of light about three feet above the top of your head. So, when you learn to experience your aura by connecting with it and cleansing it regularly, you will be able to tap into your higher self, the one that knows your true purpose, your past, present, and future, your potential, and your strengths and weaknesses.

How to Access the Intangible Systems

So, how do you connect with and strengthen these four intangible elements that play a pivotal role in your effort to connect with your guardian angels? Before you try any of the recommendations below, the first thing to know and accept is that your higher self is not in some unreachable realm. It is part of you; it has been – and will always be – part of you. To harness their power, you must only deepen your connection with these spiritual aspects.

The more you connect with your spiritual identities, the easier it is to accept and take advantage of the power of your spiritual experiences. The most common ways are meditation, visualization, and breathwork, designed to decrease the distance between your physical and spiritual identities. Let's look at each of them in a bit of detail.

Create a Sacred Space

A sacred space is where you can discover yourself repeatedly. It is a dedicated space in your home where you can do all your spiritual work, including meditation, breathwork, etc. Even if you are not yet a spiritually inclined person, a sacred space can be your quiet getaway from the noise and the hustle-bustle of daily life.

Creating a sacred space can be as simple as having a chair in a favorite spot in your home where you can sit and mull things quietly. Alternatively, it can be a space where you can light a candle, place the image or idol of your deity (if you have one), burn some incense, place a couple of crystals to keep out negativity and attract positivity, etc.

Your sacred space can also be a home for your favorite memorabilia you have collected over your lifetime. The foundation of a sacred space is that you should feel at peace and utterly comfortable in that area.

Breathwork

Breathwork involves conscious breathing techniques that help you bypass the mind to enter higher states of consciousness and awareness. Breathwork gives your brain's cognitive function something to focus on so that you can bypass the mental body and go into the spiritual, invisible realm.

There are different forms of breathwork, each with its own set of rules and unique purpose based on which you get varying effects. Breathwork techniques help you become aware of your thoughts, feelings, and memories. Here are some pointers to create your own sacred space:

First, decide what is "sacred" for you. Avoid trends and what others are doing. Ask yourself and find authentic answers aligned with your lifestyle and needs. Do you need your space to do meditation, yoga, or simply an undisturbed spot to read? If you have picked up this book, you are looking for a spiritual connection. In that case, you already know what you need your sacred space for.

Next, find a spot in your home that can become your sacred space. While an entire room is nice, you don't need one. A small corner in your home is enough. It can be the top of your dresser, a small table in your reading room, or a sunroom. Some people have their sacred space right in the middle of their living room, and you can choose one that suits you best.

Once you have found your space, create an altar. Find personal, meaningful items for your altar. For example, some people may have little miniature idols passed on from their parents or grandparents. It could be something you bought while on a trip to your favorite place of worship. It could be a gift from someone special who loves and cares for you. It could be an item that lifted you from your lowest point in life.

Place all these items neatly on a tray or a table, depending on the size of your space. Candles and incense make a lot of sense too. Lighting a candle and/or burning incense before your meditation or breathwork session sets the right mood.

Your sacred place is ready! Remember, there are no hard and fast rules to creating this space. You can do what drives and motivates you. But usually, the items mentioned above are part of any sacred space. So, now it's time to get down to how you can tap into your higher self.

Meditation

Meditation is the easiest lesson to learn but not as easy to practice. Without disciplined regularity, mastering meditation will not happen. When you meditate, you deliberately cut out all external noises and turn inward to find those elements that help you connect with the spiritual realm. It could be your aura, spiritual body, or chakras. Meditation can help quieten the noise around and within you so that you can tap into your higher self. Here is a simple meditation exercise for you to get started.

Sit in your sacred space. You will need about 10 minutes initially. As you keep practicing, you can increase the duration. Make sure all distracting elements are turned off and kept away from you.

Sit with your back erect but not too stiff. You should be relaxed and comfortable. Take a couple of deep breaths for enhanced relaxation.

Now, notice your thoughts consciously. Avoid trying to control your mind. Your mind's job is to think; therefore, trying to stop it would be counterproductive for your needs. Just be aware of each thought as it comes and goes. Suppose the first thought that you noticed was how you felt when your partner rejected you. Notice your body's reaction to this thought. Did you feel your body stiffen? Did tears come to your eyes? Did anger arise? Just observe all this without reacting or responding to them, and you will notice that thought has passed and another has taken its place.

Try and notice as many thoughts as you can. Observe every thought taking root in your mind, becoming powerful, causing reactions and responses in you, and then going away into oblivion. The same thought could return, and you merely repeat the above process for each thought.

It seems like a simple process, and yet it can be a challenge to do it. The most important thing is not to be impatient and/or unkind to yourself. Until now, your mind did as it pleased and without your awareness. Now, you are trying to become aware of your mind. Any change will have resistance, and fighting that resistance is the key to seeing what is behind the wall. Just embrace everything that comes with your thoughts, including your thoughts themselves.

As you practice this day after day, diligently and unfailingly, you will notice that you can sit for longer without becoming affected by the reactions and responses created by these thoughts. You learn to allow them without resistance, and your mind slows down enough to see each thought more clearly and impactfully than before. Thoughts do not disturb you anymore. On the contrary, they give you deep insights into the workings of your mind.

The deeper you go into your mind, the closer you go toward your higher self.

Chakra Meditation with Visualization

Use these steps to meditate successfully on your seven chakras and feel the energy in each of them flow freely throughout your body and mind.

As usual for any form of meditation, make sure you have at least 10-15 minutes of undisturbed time. You can use your sacred space or any other place that suits you. Sit comfortably, ensuring electronic notifications are all switched off.

You can do the chakra meditation while either standing up or sitting down. Close your eyes, take a few breaths to ground yourself, and then focus on the seven chakras, starting with the root chakra. If you are sitting on a chair, ensure your feet are firmly placed on the ground. Your body must be connected to the earth.

Root chakra - Bring your focus to the base of your spine. Imagine a red disc or wheel of light spinning at the root chakra's location. Imagine this red light connecting your body firmly to the earth through your feet. As you breathe in, visualize drawing positive vibes from the earth into your root chakra. As you breathe out, visualize sending off all negative vibes from your body into the earth. When you feel satisfied, move to the sacral chakra.

Sacral chakra – Focus on the point two inches below your navel, where the sacral chakra is located. Imagine a bright orange disc or wheel spinning in that location. As you breathe in, visualize energy being drawn from the ocean into your body. As you breathe out, visualize all the negative energy leaving your body to be absorbed into the mighty ocean. Keep focusing on the sacral chakra until you feel cleansed of all negative emotions.

Remember, the red disc of the root chakra is still spinning even if your attention is not on it. Now visualize a tube of red light from there reaching up to the navel and connecting itself to the orange disc.

Navel chakra - Focus on the solar plexus imagining a yellow ball of fire spinning at the location. As you breathe in, visualize the fire burning away all the blocks and negativity from your body. You can visualize the smoke from the burned negativity finding its way to your nostrils and leaving your system as you exhale. Visualize the tube of orange and red moving up and connecting itself to the solar plexus's yellow ball of fire.

Heart chakra - As you move up to the heart chakra, visualize a disc of green light spinning at the center of your chest, the location of the Anahata. As you breathe in, visualize love filling up the green disc. Imagine this love permeating every part of your body. As you breathe out, visualize hate, resentment, jealousy, and all other emotions opposing your love and compassion for yourself being exhaled out of your system. Finally, imagine the red-orange-yellow tube from the chakras beneath rising up to connect itself with the green disc of the heart chakra.

Throat chakra - As you move up to the throat chakra, move your head around in a circle (5 counts anticlockwise and 5 counts clockwise) to relax the neck area. Focus on the area of your throat, imaging a blue disc spinning there, empowering you to identify and stand by your authenticity.

Visualizing the blue light emerging out of your ears also helps you be a good listener. Imagine the power of written and vocal communication entering your system as you breathe in and visualize all the blockages of communication leaving your system as you exhale. Imagine that tube mixed with the red, orange, yellow, and green of the previous four chakras rising up and connecting itself to the blue of your throat chakra.

Third eye chakra - Meditating on the third eye expands your mind and helps deepen your connection with your intuition. Meditating on the 6th important chakra helps you break limiting barriers that prevent you from connecting with your higher self. Focus on the space between your eyebrows and visualize a disc of indigo spinning there. Just focus gently on this space allowing all the thoughts to come and go.

Visualize your thoughts escaping into the black nothingness, leaving you peaceful and calm. Try and capture the glimpses of light coming from the innermost being of your soul between these thoughts. Keep your breath steady and smooth as you visualize the tube mixed with six colors rising to the third eye and connecting itself with the indigo.

Crown chakra - This energy vortex will help you tap into your higher self. Imagine a thousand-petalled lotus at this vortex. Invite this flower to open itself to you. Visualize a purple or violet column of light on top of your head. Visualize this violet column of light moving down toward your body and up toward the sky with every inhalation and exhalation.

This violet column of light is the Divine consciousness. Next, visualize that tube connecting all the six previous chakras rising up to connect with the thousand-petalled lotus. Visualize the petals opening up and giving you access to all the cosmic energy. Imagine your entire being filled with this limitless cosmic energy.

The trick with chakras is that the energy of all seven of them has to be unified before you can harness the power of the 6th and 7th chakras, two of the most useful energy centers to connect with your higher self through which you can access the invisible, spiritual realm. So, randomly picking one chakra to meditate on may help you deal with the elements connected with the chosen energy vortex, even if compromised.

For a complete, wholesome makeover in your energy field, it is vital that you start from the root chakra and successively move up until the seven colors combine and burst into the white light beyond the crown chakra, the energy center with direct access to the realm of your guardian angels.

Journaling

Journaling is also an easy and effective way to connect with your higher self. Writing down your thoughts and feelings gives you an objective perspective without attachment. Consequently, you find ideas and solutions to hidden problems.

Journaling helps you reach deep into your consciousness and find your deepest desires and dreams. It helps you connect with your authenticity and your true purpose as the external layers of thoughts and complexity of the outside world are peeled away slowly but surely through journaling. Here are some prompts for your journey to your higher self:

- **Who am I?** - The answers to this question can start with something as simple as your name, occupation, and address. Slowly include what you think is your personality, your responses to various stimuli, and how you handle happiness, sadness, anger, etc.
- **What are your desires?**
- **What are the three biggest lessons you have learned in your life until now?** How will you apply those lessons in your current life?
- **What are the desires you have yet to fulfill?** After writing them down, see if those desires look as desirable as before. Do you want to change them? If yes, how?
- **What takes up most of your time and energy?** Are they aligned with your dreams?
- **If all your desires are fulfilled, what plans do you have for your life?** What's left?
- **If you could eliminate all kinds of fear, including the fear of death, what would be the first thing you would do?**
- **What gives you unconditional joy?** Why?

Use the above prompts to start your journey into journaling. The more you write, the more you need to dig deep into your mind, and the closer you will get to your higher self.

Working with Crystals

Crystals have been formed on and under the Earth's surface over millions of years. Every crystal has a unique molecular formation holding the vibrations captured over the million years they took to transform into their present state. Crystals hold ancient energy and wisdom existing from prehistoric times.

Ancient wise men understood and appreciated the power of crystals used for thousands of years for their medicinal and healing properties. Being drawn to a particular crystal is not limited to its physical beauty but also to its vibrational frequency, which may match yours.

Crystals serve different psychological, physiological, and spiritual purposes, including but not limited to the following:

- Amethyst is used to get rid of bad habits
- Kyanite is great for deep emotional healing
- Clear quartz helps you restore balance and harmony in your life

And some crystals help you tap into your higher self. You can hold them in your hand as you meditate or put them on the altar in your sacred space. Here are some crystals which are great for increased spiritual vitality:

- **Clear quartz** is a soul cleanser and improves clarity. It helps you clear your thoughts and connect with your true life purpose. It is also great to enhance the power of your intention and to manifest your desires. It is a highly useful crystal for all types of healing, including physical, mental, and spiritual ailments.
- **Lapis lazuli** is a stone for vision and wisdom. It helps stimulate your mind's higher and deeper faculties to enhance spiritual experiences. It promotes self-expression as it empowers you to confront your inner truths.
- **Labradorite** has strong connections with the spiritual realm. It helps you raise your consciousness and boost your intuitive powers and psychic abilities.
- **Kyanite** is an excellent crystal for dealing with resentment and anger, especially those that confuse and confound you and prevent you from connecting with your true inner self. It amplifies high-frequency energies to heighten your psychic and intuitive powers.
- **Amethyst** is great to use in third-eye meditation. It offers the power of spiritual awakening while soothing emotional and mental disturbances.

To summarize, tapping into your higher self plays an important role in connecting with your guardian angels. The more you dig deep into your psyche to connect with your higher self, the one with direct access to the ultimate cosmic truth, the easier it will be to access the power and guidance of your guardian angels. These invisible, spiritual beings are waiting for your connection to help and guide you as much as you want to reach out to them.

Chapter Three: Communicating with Your Guardian Angel

The previous chapter dealt with tapping into your higher self to connect with the invisible, spiritual realm where the guardian angels usually reside. This chapter deals with communicating with your guardian angels, identifying and interpreting the signs they send you, and following their guidance.

Guardian angels are divine, spiritual beings. They do not use human language for communication and have their own ways of interacting and communicating with you. If you need to understand them, you need to learn their language. The more you connect with your higher self, the more your ability will be to read the subtle signs that your guardian angels are sending you.

Guardian angels constantly communicate with humans, guiding them, teaching them to discern right from wrong, and sending warning signals. They use various types of signals to connect with people. It is easy to miss these signals in the hustle and bustle of your daily life. Sometimes, you see the signals but don't understand the signs because your higher self-connection is weak and may even trivialize them.

Guardian angels can send warning signs to humans.
https://www.pexels.com/photo/close-up-photo-of-caution-signage-4447140/

Guardian angels can also use your inner voice to guide you. Often, you get so lost in your daily life that you don't see danger signs. Guardian angels can send you warnings by speaking to you as your inner voice. You have to remain conscious and stay present to catch these signs and follow their lead.

Sarah was going through a bad phase in life. She lost her job thanks to the economic slowdown and job cuts. Her long-term relationship with Joe had ended recently, and she realized he was cheating on her with his colleague. She was struggling to keep her sanity. Her best friend, Susan, tried to help her as much as she could. But Sarah was drowning in a pool of depression.

One day, Susan decided to introduce her to the concept and belief in guardian angels. It was a long and difficult conversation but worth it.

Susan: *"If you don't get out of your mire of sadness and depression soon, you'll fall into it irretrievably."*

Sarah: *"How can I, Susan? It's so difficult to cope with all this, and I'm so alone."*

Susan: *"None of us is ever alone, Sarah. We always have our guardian angel with us, right from birth until we leave this world. This angel guides us through our lives, lighting our path in times of darkness."*

Sarah: *"What rubbish! If this so-called guardian angel exists, why doesn't she help me now?"*

Susan: *"She is helping you. You choose to ignore her."*

Sarah: *"How can I ignore someone when I don't even know of her existence?"*

Susan: *"Exactly! Now that I've told you about her, can you reach out and seek her help?"*

Sarah: *"How can I reach out if she is not visible?"*

Susan: *"Open your heart and mind to her help, and she will find a way to reach out to you."*

Susan then explained to Sarah how guardian angels work, and with a little bit of persistence, Sarah found her guardian angel, who helped her deal with all her problems by showing her solutions and answers, which Sarah had not been able to see until then. Her life has improved considerably now. She converted her love for embroidery into an income-generating hobby, and she is not only financially independent but has also come to terms with her broken relationship with Joe, moving on to find new love.

There are two parts to this chapter. The first part is how you can reach out and seek answers and guidance from your guardian angels. The second part of this chapter deals with reading the signs your guardian angel is sending out to you.

Communicating with Guardian Angels

Here are some pointers to help you communicate with your guardian angels:

Know Your Guardian Angel's Name

First, learn their names. Yes, you can find out the name of your guardian angel, especially if you are getting closer to your higher self. Remember, the angel is as keen on communicating with you as you are with her. Use these steps to find out the name(s) of your guardian angel:

Sit with your eyes closed in your sacred space. Relax completely, ensuring that all disturbances, including the energies from other people and things, are blocked out. When you are relaxed and ready, ask your higher self the name(s) of your guardian angel. The name will come to you in some way or another. You could get it as a sign (discussed in the next section of this chapter), or the name could be placed seemingly inexplicably in your head. Even if nothing comes to you in your first sitting, try again, and sooner or later, the name of your guardian angel will be revealed to you.

It could be that even after a few sittings, the name is not being given to you. In that case, your guardian angel likely wants you to give her a name. Pick a cherished name, a name that makes you happy and secure. Say the name out loud and see if you feel happy and warm when you say it. Make a note of this name and begin to address your guardian angels by the name you hear or have given them.

Once you have named them, ask them to send you a signal that they are there for you, always. You can ask this question either through meditation, making an entry in your journal, or prayer. Once you have asked the question, keep your eyes peeled for the signs or signals from your guardian angel.

Dedicate a Song to Your Guardian Angel

Dedicate a song to them. Once your first connection with your guardian angel is set, the next thing you need to do is have a calling card for them. There is nothing like a song as a personal dedication to them. Take a favorite song and tell your guardian angel that this is theirs. Whenever you play or sing it, it means that you want to connect with them. The reverse is also true. If you hear the song playing somewhere without you having set it in motion, it could mean your guardian angel is there for your protection and safety.

Write Letters

You can write letters to them. Start with, "My dear guardian angel..." and proceed to write whatever is bothering you. This works well if you are stuck in an uncertain situation and cannot decide which choice is good for you. At such times, write to your guardian angel explaining your predicament and then look out for signs from them to help you make a choice.

Angel Meditation

Angelic meditation helps you communicate with your guardian angel. Use these steps:

- Sit comfortably in your sacred space or any other place that is free of disturbances.
- Turn off the electric lights and light a candle.

- Breathe slowly and deeply for a minute to relax completely, ensuring your entire body is calm and relaxed.
- You can recite a pre-written prayer to your guardian angel during your meditation session.
- Alternatively, you can call their name and speak to them, and you can do so out loud or in your mind.
- Imagine your guardian angel sitting close to you, teaching and guiding you.
- Sit in this state for a few minutes until you are satisfied that you have conveyed your message to your guardian angel.
- Finally, give them your gratitude and open your eyes slowly. Let the candle burn until the end.
- Now, wait for your guardian angel to respond to your prayer.

Visualize Your Guardian Angel

You can easily visualize your guardian angel using a mirror – here are those steps:

Sit comfortably in front of a mirror, opening your heart and mind for the encounter with a heavenly being.

Turn off all artificial lights in the room and light a couple of candles.

1. Close your eyes and breathe deeply and slowly for about 2 minutes until you feel totally relaxed and calm.
2. Send a prayer, asking for guidance to see your guardian angel.
3. Now, open your eyes and look at yourself in the mirror.
4. Notice the calmness and peace on your face and body.
5. Then slowly say, *"You are, I know, my dear guardian angel, always by my side. From the heavenly realm to mine as commanded by Him. You are my protector, my guardian, and my guide. Reveal yourself to me."*

Keep repeating this prayer staring deeply into your eyes in the mirror, ensuring your breathing is relaxed and calm. Look deeper and deeper into your eyes. Slowly, your guardian angel will be revealed to you as a reflection in the mirror. It will start with your aura appearing in the mirror first, and then this aura will change shape to form your angel. Embrace your guardian with an open heart full of love. Send gratitude to Him and thank your angel for appearing before you.

Wait until the form disappears, then blow out the candle and switch on the lights in the room. Sit quietly for a few minutes, absorbing the heavenly feeling of seeing your guardian angel before you return to the human world.

Interpreting the Signs of Guardian Angels

Your guardian angel sends you messages (answers to your questions, guidance, or even warning signals) through different kinds of signs. Let's look in detail at some of these signals:

Angel Numbers

Angel numbers are signs from the spiritual world carrying a message for those who see them. Have you looked at your phone and found that the time reads 1:11 or 2:22, or 3:33? You have just listened to your favorite song that is 2 minutes 22 seconds long while sitting in a cafe. You call for the bill and find the total is $2.22! What are these numbers? Repetitive numbers, usually repeated three or four times, make you stop and look at them with wonder.

In addition to their enchantingly symbolic meaning, these special numbers are also seen as angelic messages sent to people from their spiritual friends. These angelic or special numbers offer insight and wisdom and indicate the path to be taken.

Angel numbers are different from other numbers in numerology because they are not directly connected with your personality. These numbers have nothing to do with your birth charts, astrological and/or zodiac signs, or life path number. Also, they can appear anywhere at any time. They can show up on clocks and watches (as already discussed above), timestamps, receipts, bills, license plates, phone numbers, and other day-to-day elements you encounter daily.

The reason for their appearances in seemingly ordinary objects is that it is a way for the divine will to intentionally show you what you need to know. These numbers can be gentle reminders that there is something greater and bigger than you see and experience, and it is from that One who is running this world. He has your back and will always have it.

The meaning of each of these angel numbers discussed below is very personal and could be interpreted differently depending on the context. For example, for one person, the number 333 could mean that they should follow their instincts, and for someone else, it could mean that they are on the right track. With practice, connecting the angel numbers you see with your current life scenario, you will learn to discern their meanings accurately. It's worth looking at some of these numbers to understand their significance.

Zero - The number zero represents new opportunities and new beginnings. If you see a pattern of zeroes (in threes (000), fours (0000), or a pattern that stands out within a bigger number), then it could mean the start of something new. It could be interpreted that you are at the start of a new cycle or phase in your life. The sighting of this number tells you that you should not be afraid to make bold decisions as it is a time for new opportunities and beginnings.

One - Number one is a powerful symbol and is believed to be the go-ahead message from the spiritual world. Suppose you see a pattern of ones (111 or 1111 or any other unique pattern). In that case, you should quickly make a wish, set an intention, or sow a seed because whatever you do, the cosmos will be aligned with your actions and help you achieve it. Seeing a pattern of number 1 means you are getting the unconditional support of guardian angels and other spiritual beings.

Two - Number two stands for alignment, trust, and balance. Suppose you see a unique pattern of twos (222, 2222, or any other pattern). In that case, it means that your guardian angel is doing everything possible to help you get where you want to go. If you see twos in patterns, then you should try reaching out to someone you trust because He will make the collaboration fruitful.

Three - Three stands for creativity, and if you see the number three in a specific and/or repetitive pattern (333, 3333, or any other pattern), it is time to enhance your unique skills and talent. The appearance of three means the skill you will learn will enhance your value in your current life situation, personally or professionally. Number three is telling you that your creativity is vital.

Four - Number four stands for stability. If you see the number four in repetitive patterns (444, 4444, or any other sequence), then it indicates that you are building a strong structure rooted and grounded so well that it will be a legacy. Seeing number four in angelic patterns means you are navigating through a long-term project that cannot be built on your own. Therefore, sighting number four also means you should not hesitate to ask for assistance from well-intentioned, knowledgeable, and like-minded people.

Five - Seeing the number five in angelic patterns (555 or 5555) could indicate a big shift on the horizon. If you have been trapped, stifled, and caught in a rut, then the sighting of patterned fives means something big is in the offing, and that underground and foundational work toward that end is happening as of now. By showing you fives in a pattern, your guardian angel is telling you that you are on the right path and that patience will give you great rewards.

Six - Contrary to popular religious associations with the number six (666 is referred to as the devil's number!), the angelic number six stands for compassion and support. When you see six in repetitive (666 or 6666) or unique patterns in your vision, it is a gentle reminder that you need self-care and self-compassion. Even if things are not going according to your needs and wants, your guardian angel is sending you a signal to treat yourself with kindness and compassion. Six is a reminder that everything happens for a reason.

Seven - Number seven stands for good fortune. Seeing this number in patterns (777 or 7777) indicates good fortune financially is on its way to you. It could indicate new monetarily lucrative and income-generating opportunities. Number seven exhorts you to explore business ventures outside your comfort zone.

Eight - Eight is one of the most divine numbers in numerology. If you see the number eight in repetition or any other pattern (888, 8888, or any other sequence), it indicates a strong connection to spirituality. It could mean that someone from the afterlife is watching out for you. Eight is also a symbol of infinity, the interconnected, unending loop representing the limitlessness of life and the universe. It indicates that you must not be afraid to dig deep into your intuition and do what you have to do.

Nine - The number nine symbolizes the end of a cycle or chapter in your life. Seeing the number nine in an angelic pattern (999, 9999, or any other pattern) could indicate that a cycle or phase of your life is coming to a meaningful end and that you should be prepared for new beginnings. When you see number nine, it also means it is time to step outside your comfort zone and explore new opportunities, especially now that the previous cycle is coming to an end.

Cloud Formations

Cloud formations and shapes have symbolic meanings in every culture, and the reason for this is that angels and other divine beings use clouds to send messages to humans. Here are some important cloud formations and their significance.

Cumulus clouds - The fluffy, white appearance of cumulus clouds resembling cotton candy and marshmallows signifies hope and innocence. Seen in the sky during springtime, cumulus clouds symbolize new beginnings as well. They can also remind you to stay positive and keep doing what you need to do, and things will certainly fall into place sooner rather than later.

The sight of beautiful cumulus clouds was the first ray of hope that Susan, who was struggling to believe in guardian angels, got from her guardian angel. Her outlook on life changed, and with it came happiness and hope. So, the next time you see cumulus clouds, let them remind you to take a pause from life, enjoy their beauty, and look forward to a hopeful, brighter future. It is a sign from your guardian angel.

Stratus clouds - Stratus clouds block out the sun making the day dull and gloomy signifying impending unpleasant situations. If you feel down on a gray day, thanks to the unhelpful stratus clouds, do an outdoor activity or indulge in your favorite hobby, and you will feel better. Your guardian angel is also telling you to stay low during this time of gloom and despair.

Cirrus clouds - Symbolize change and transition. If you see cirrus clouds during a changing phase in your life, your guardian angel tells you that you are on the right path. Also, cirrus clouds bring happiness and good fortune.

Cumulonimbus clouds - These clouds signify power and strength. They are large, flat-bottomed clouds associated with extreme weather conditions and are harbingers of heavy rains, storms, and even tornadoes. When you see these clouds, your guardian angel may be giving you warnings of an upcoming storm in your life.

Altocumulus clouds - The sightings of these clouds mean something good is on its way to you. They represent balance and harmony and remind you that regardless of what is happening in your life, you must keep your chin up and remain grounded and positive. Good things are on the way.

Lenticular clouds - These cloud formations are bizarre yet beautiful. They signify mystery and magic and appear to hover in the sky like giant saucers. In some cultures, it is believed that angels and spirits live in lenticular clouds. In the world of angels, seeing lenticular clouds could be an indication that something important is about to happen in your life.

Nimbostratus clouds - These low-level, dark, and foreboding clouds signify grief and sadness. They generally precede rain or snow and could also indicate the coming of hope and happiness, even if the current situation involves grief.

Stratocumulus clouds - These horizontal, low, and gray clouds are associated with comfort and security. Often seen in the morning or evening, stratocumulus clouds could bring in a light shower. Feeling fearful and anxious and seeing stratocumulus clouds in the sky could be a sign of comfort and security from your guardian angel.

Cirrostratus clouds - These awe-inspiring clouds signify spirituality and intuition. These delicate, wispy clouds are often mistaken for cirrus clouds. However, cirrostratus clouds are larger, more spread out, thinner, and more uniform in shape than cirrus clouds. When you see cirrostratus clouds, you can be sure that they are a sign of happiness and good fortune from your guardian angel.

Dreams and Visions

The primary difference between dreams and visions is that the latter is manifested in a waking state, while the former is seen when you are asleep. And yet, when people have visions, their five senses are so deeply affected that they are almost unconscious and oblivious to the ordinary happenings around them. Your guardian angel may appear to you while you are talking to someone and give you visions of what will soon transpire.

Visions can be in the form of sparkles of light, hazy (unclear or clear) forms, or absolutely clear pictures and images. These visions often come suddenly and without warning as you go about your daily work. The flashes of light or a glimpse of a glowing figure which resembles an angel may become visible to you. But when you try to look directly at these visions, they can simply disappear.

If you are getting these visions and dreams more than before, your sensitivity to your guardian angel's presence is improving. You could not notice them before, but now you are at least catching glimpses of their form and the vision they are trying to send you.

The same logic holds good for dreams too. If your guardian angel is trying to send you a message through your dreams, then you must pay attention to your dreams and try to interpret them. Start a dream journal and make detailed notes of your dreams every night. The more you connect with your dreams, the easier it will be for you to interpret your guardian angel's messages.

Physical Sensations and Emotions

Quite often, you may have felt a sudden, inexplicable tingling sensation in your body, and quite frequently, you will have dismissed it as something random and unimportant. Now that you know that divine beings from the spiritual realms communicate differently with you, *don't repeat your earlier mistakes.*

The physical sensations could be connected to sudden changes in the temperature or the environment. You may feel warm because it's become inexplicably sunnier, or you could feel cold because there is a sudden nip in the air unexpectedly and without reason or logic.

If you feel this kind of physical sensation, stop and try to understand it better. What did you think before you felt that sensation? Was something worrying you? Or were you wondering how to solve a dilemma? Your guardian angel is always around and already knows your problems.

The angel may not wait for you to seek their help, and they may choose to send you a message without you asking for it. Therefore, you will interpret the sign correctly when you deeply ponder what triggered the sensation. For example, suppose you have had a bad breakup recently, and you are wondering if it is time for you to get over it and move on, and that thought was in your head just before that tingling sensation. It could mean your guardian angel is giving you the go-ahead.

In this way, physical sensations and emotions are used by guardian angels to send you messages.

Feathers

Your guardian angel could use feathers to communicate with you. Suppose you find feathers appearing out of nowhere. In that case, you can safely assume your guardian angel is aware of your situation and there to help you. Feathers are her gift for you. Different colored feathers have different meanings. Here are some examples:

- A white feather signifies a message from your recently deceased loved ones that they are fine and that they are watching over you.

- A brown feather can be interpreted as stability in your domestic life
- A red feather represents courage, vitality, good fortune, and passion
- A yellow feather reminds you to harness the power of your intelligence and mental acuity
- A green feather is a sign of abundance, fertility, and growth
- An orange feather signifies the power of your sexuality, sensuality, and creativity

Unusual Scents

Guardian angels use scents to send you messages too. Flower scents are the most common way for angels and spirits to communicate with you. If you smell a flower scent when there are no flowers, it could be a message from your guardian angel. Rose scent is specifically powerful because it vibrates at the highest rate among all flower scents. Flower scents have different meanings. Some examples are as follows:

- **Rose** - Encouragement, security, and comfort
- **Mint** - Purity
- **Frankincense** - Spiritual enlightenment
- **Spruce** - Joy
- **Cinnamon** - Peace
- **Grapefruit** - Gratitude

Other scents used include the memorable smell of a loved one, a pet, etc. It could be the scent of your favorite place, hometown, or home. It could be the scent of a food item you love or a dish your mother always prepared to lift your spirits.

Human and Animal Messengers

Your guardian angel may use other human beings and/or animals to send you messages. For example, you could have asked your angel for help or advice concerning some trouble brewing in the office, and as soon as you sit at your desk, your colleague could say something that would be the answer you were seeking all along.

Here's another scenario explaining how guardian angels use animals to communicate with you. Again, suppose you sought help or advice from your guardian angel regarding some issue in your life. And suddenly, you see an animal you feel drawn to without rhyme or reason. You may want to look up the spiritual significance of sighting the animal. A chapter later on in this book deals with animal guides and helpers.

What are the guardian angels trying to tell you? The answer to this is personal and dependent on what you seek. Often their messages could have the following meanings:

I am with you - Through one of the signs mentioned above, your guardian angel may allay your fears and insecurities. They could tell you that you are not alone, that she is there with you through thick and thin, and that things will be fine.

Be careful - Sometimes, the message could be a warning, and it could ask you to be careful about something. It could be directed at one of your life choices or be a warning about something going wrong soon – something you are not fully focused on.

Communicating with your guardian angel does not have to be only when you need them. You can meditate or visualize their presence at any time. You can talk to them as you would talk to your best friend. You can share your thoughts and ideas with them and let them know everything about your life. It is not that they don't know what is happening in your life. After all, they are by your side right from birth.

Yet, talking to them and telling them everything is a great way to use your free will and align your purpose with the divine will. When you speak to your guardian angel, you acknowledge their presence in your life and show Him your gratitude for this dedicated being in your life, which has happened only because of His command.

Chapter Four: Working with the Archangels

In Greek, the word *"archangel"* translates to *"the chief of angels.* As you already know, archangels belong to the higher ranks and are believed to manage guardian angels. You read about archangels and their roles in brief in an earlier chapter. Many archangels are mentioned in Christianity, Islam, and Judaism. In this book, you will learn more about the four most important archangels and their significance in the spiritual world.

The Almighty God has created the four archangels to be in charge of the four cardinal directions on Earth. This is so the balanced energy of the four archangels in the four directions facilitates humankind to lead a life according to God's will. Uriel is for the north, Michael is for the south, Raphael is for the east, and Gabriel is for the west.

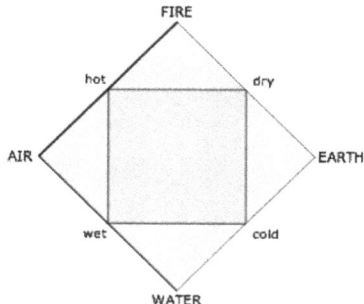

The archangels are in charge of the four elements.
https://commons.wikimedia.org/wiki/File:Four_elements_representation.svg

Further, He put each of his four important archangels in charge of the four elements, namely earth, fire, air, and water, as follows:

- Raphael for air
- Michael for fire
- Gabriel for water
- Uriel for earth

Archangel Michael

His name means "*He who is God-like*" and is concerned with truth and justice. As you already know, he is the most important archangel and the epitome of courage, strength, and power. He is the archangel you should reach out to when you feel drained of all energy, and he will help get rid of negative energies in your life. He is the protector of all those who love God.

Michael holds a flaming sword and a shield, both depicting him as a commander. He is sometimes seen holding a set of scales representing him as an angel of justice, delivering that justice swiftly and keenly. Like the element of fire which he governs, Michael helps you burn away your sins to prepare you for the path of spirituality.

Archangel Michael keeps you safe from all kinds of dangers. Call upon him before starting a journey to keep you safe from accidents and mishaps. He is the archangel to call upon when facing a crisis, and he is known to communicate with his seekers boldly. So, in the middle of a crisis (if you have already sought the help of Archangel Michael), you may hear a powerful voice giving you advice, telling you the right thing to do. Sometimes, you may experience a warm, tingling sensation that makes you feel secure and comfortable. Get to recognize this feeling as signifying the presence of this protecting angel by your side.

The colors representing Archangel Michael are royal purple, royal blue, or gold. So, in visions, he may appear as a purple haze, or you could see a blue or gold aura before you hear his words of advice. The presence of Archangel Michael is usually unmistakable. He does not hesitate to make himself and his presence known to seekers.

The primary purpose of Archangel Michael is to help you lead an organized and productive life so that you can fulfill God's purpose. To this end, Michael helps you learn supporting skills and develop your God-given talents.

The crystal of Archangel Michael is sugilite which comes in varied colors ranging from violet to magenta. Sugilite is also known as Luvulite and Royal Azel. Archangel Michael is also associated with amethyst, topaz, and clear quartz. With his sword of truth and scale of justice, he is associated with the throat chakra. Gluttony is one of the worst outcomes of an unbalanced throat chakra, a vice where you only take and do not give. Also, gluttony is manifested in the form of harsh and unkind words. Archangel Michael helps to balance this justice.

Archangel Michael rules over the sun, his weekday is Sunday, the day of relaxation, and his number is 11. Here is a simple prayer to Archangel Michael. Say it when you need his help, and he will reveal himself through his royal purple color and give you the necessary guidance and help.

"Archangel Michael, protect me from the snares of evil, the wickedness in the world. Keep me safe from the evil effects of Satan. I beseech you to ask God on my behalf to cast all negativity into Hell. I pray for clarity and strength to walk the path He has chosen for me."

Archangel Raphael

The meaning of the word Raphael is *"God who heals."* Archangel Raphael is known as the Master Healer and is associated with the heart chakra. When the energy in your heart chakra is free-flowing and balanced, then your life will be filled with love and light.

Seek his help if you are facing obstacles in finding your soulmate because he is the angel of matchmaking. He will balance your heart chakra and help you discover your true love. Like the element of air that he governs, Archangel Raphael helps you to break away from burdens that are holding your soul back. He helps you lighten the soul so that it can rise to meet the divine.

Archangel Raphael shows you the path toward self-healing, and with a healthy body, mind, and spirit, you can do wonders in your life. You can call upon Archangel Raphael for your emotional, mental, and physical healing. The Master Healer often communicates using his signature green light, the light that heals. He is also the patron angel of the sick and all healers, including modern-day physicians, medical practitioners, and conventional alternative healers.

He is also the angel to call upon before embarking on any journey. He ensures smooth travel without delays and problems. He also represents youth. He is depicted as a young man in traveling clothes, holding a staff in his hand and a fish. He is known to have healed a blind man with the help of the fish.

Archangel Raphael's day is Wednesday. He is the ruler of Mercury, and his gemstones are green agate, emerald, and yellow calcite. The scents he uses to connect with you are sandalwood, chamomile, and lemongrass.

He can send you messages through sparks of green light, tingles of warmth or chills, a premonition through dreams, and a sudden love for nature and the outdoors. Here's a little prayer that you can use to seek Archangel Raphael's help.

"Dear Archangel Raphael, watch over our health and protect us from disease and illness. Make me a healthy vessel to carry out His will. Please send me counsel and guidance on love and finding a soulmate. Help my heart to make the right decision."

Archangel Uriel

Uriel translates to *"God's light."* He is the preserver and protector of humanity. He is the angel of insight, information, learning, truth, wisdom, and ideas. He is the patron angel of teachers and students. He is the angel you will call upon when you are stuck for ideas or need a solution for a particularly problematic issue in your life. Like the element earth, which he represents, Gabriel Uriel grounds you to solid reliability that comes with following God's path.

Archangel Uriel is associated with the root chakra, which deals with grounding and stability. Call upon this angel to allay your fears and uncertainties and to help you ground your energy through the root chakra. Archangel Uriel's day is Friday. His colors are orange and/or gold. He is the ruler of the Sun and the symbol of light and the stars.

Archangel Uriel connects with you when you are serving others. He will not hesitate to tell you the truth, no matter how bitter or frightful it is. Knowing the truth is the first step toward making positive changes. He is depicted holding a sword and a book, both of which stand for wisdom.

He communicates in different ways, including sending red sparks of light (red is his color) through dreams and through electricity (because he sparks your mind). If you find your bulb flickering suddenly, then it could mean that Archangel Uriel is showering his blessings on you or sending you a message.

He is associated with number 1, the number of self-growth and learning. So, if you see 111 or 1111, it is an indication of Archangel Uriel's presence. The gemstones associated with the "angel of light" are amber, fire opal, and basalt. Here is a prayer you can use to call upon Archangel Uriel.

> *"Dear Archangel Uriel, please give me clarity. I'm confused and worried. Light up my path so that I can see into the darkest corners for insights and wisdom. Give me the strength to look the truth in the eye and deal with it without fear or embarrassment."*

Archangel Gabriel

Gabriel means *"messenger of God."* Remember, he was the one who brought the message to Mary that she would be blessed to become the mother of Lord Jesus. He works closely with children and childbirth. He is the angel you pray to for safe pregnancies and deliveries, conception, adoption, and parenting. If you face problems while dealing with your children, seek Archangel Gabriel's counsel.

Archangel Gabriel is associated with the crown chakra, the energy center with direct access to the divine realm. The pure white light of Archangel Gabriel will help you connect with divinity through inspiration, clarity of thought, and peaceful joy. This angel will help clear egotism and pride, rendering your soul perfectly pure to embrace divinity in all its glory.

Gabriel is known to help even prophets to gain clarity and vision in their search for truth and closeness with Him. Water, the element which Archangel Gabriel governs, is connected with emotions and thoughts. He helps you deal with your emotions and thoughts to find the truth you seek.

The color of Archangel Gabriel is pure white which stands for honesty, purity, unity, and peace. His symbol is the trumpet, perfectly aligned with his role as the divine messenger. He is the patron of expression and communication-based arts and crafts such as social media, mass media, journalism, clairvoyance, and other methods of truth-seeking and authenticity. He carries a scroll and scepter as he is the patron angel in hand-related arts such as painting, writing, etc.

He communicates with you in different ways. For example, suppose you feel a sudden urge to take action on an idea you have been having for a long time. In that case, it is highly likely that Archangel Gabriel is the motivator behind your action. If you have doubts about your creativity, level of skills, the relevance of your value and contribution to what you are doing, or whether you should follow your passion, seek advice from the messenger of god. He will show you the path leading to the manifestation of your deep passion.

Archangel Gabriel is associated with different crystals, including Moldavite, Citrine, Angelite, and Herkimer Diamond. He is associated with Monday as he is the ruler of the moon. Here is a small prayer you can use to pray to and seek the blessings and advice of Archangel Gabriel.

> *"Dear Archangel Gabriel, I pray for clarity of thought and the power to express my creativity without fear. Help me find the light to manifest my ideas aligned with His will. Inspire my intuition, help me deepen my connection with my instincts, and help me trust my innate power, His gift to me in this life."*

Here is a nighttime Jewish prayer called Krias Shema, which seeks protection from the four archangels.

> *"Dear God, Almighty, Bless me that Archangel Michael is on my right, Archangel Gabriel is on my left, Archangel Raphael is in front of me, and Archangel Uriel is behind me, all of them keeping me safe. Bless me so that You are always above me."*

Zodiac Signs and Archangels

In addition to the four primary archangels discussed above, the 12 zodiac signs are connected with 12 archangels (including the primary four). When you were born on this Earth, the stars and planets were aligned in a particularly unique fashion. When you try to read and interpret the positions of these planets and stars with each other and in relation to your birth, you will get deep insights into your personality and the destiny you are meant to fulfill in your life.

Mainstream media focuses on solar astrology based on your birth month. This aspect gives you only an inkling of your personality and destiny. Traditional astrology is connected to your birth chart or natal chart, which is drawn based on the position of the planets at the precise time of your birth. When read correctly, this natal chart gives you an accurate picture of your personality and the destiny you need to fulfill.

Traditional astrology helps you understand your personality traits, why you behave the way you do, and what corrective measures you can take to lead a more meaningful and purposeful life than before. Learning about your zodiac sign and its corresponding archangel can help you get the right start to delve deep into your natal chart.

This section deals with the 12 archangels associated with the solar astrology-based zodiac signs, which are, in turn, based on the birth month. The twelve zodiac signs are:

Aries

People born between March 21 and April 20 fall under the Aries zodiac sign, whose guardian is Archangel Ariel, the healing angel of nature. People born under the Aries sign are also often nature lovers and selfless human beings. They are full of creative ideas, ably supported by their patron archangel.

Ariel means "Lion (or Lioness) of God," and he protects and preserves wild plant and animal life, especially in the wild. Archangel Ariel helps you connect deeply with nature and its beauty.

For anything connected with nature, including trying for a job in the environmental science industry or setting up a garden at home, call upon Archangel Ariel for help. He is also the angel who overlooks the fairy world, home to fairies, leprechauns, and elves.

Archangel Ariel is also the angel who can help you reach self-actualization (your full potential). He drives you to dig deep within yourself and discover your true purpose in life – and then helps you find a way to achieve it. He is associated with the color pink and often makes his presence felt by pink light or sparks. Use pink quartz crystal to meditate on her and seek his help.

Taurus

People born between April 21 and May 21 are Taureans, and their governing angel is Archangel Chamuel, also referred to as "the finding angel." He helps you find lost things, and he is the one to reach out to when you are disturbed and want peace and harmony in your life.

His name means *"One who seeks God."* Seeking and finding your own divinity is the ultimate step to discovering peace and harmony within and outside of yourself. You can find Archangel Chamuel and his army of angels hovering over all places of worship. He and his angels carry your prayers to God and return with His responses.

He makes personal and professional relationships work harmoniously and without conflicts. If you want improved relationships in your personal and/or professional life, Archangel Chamuel is the one you should seek. He reveals himself as a streak or ray of pink light. Like their patron angel, Taureans are hardworking and organized, ensuring everything is done in an organized way.

Gemini

People whose birthdays fall between May 22 and June 21 are Geminis, whose governing angel is Archangel Zadkiel, the angel of righteousness, forgiveness, and memory. His memory power is legendary, and he knows for sure that everything comes from and goes into the divine will.

Forgiveness is a vital aspect of personal growth and development. Forgiving yourself facilitates forgiving others and is the first step toward building a compassionate attitude. With the help of Archangel Zadkiel, you can face and deal with troubling memories and hurtful emotions. When you are able to get over your haunting past, you will find the strength to build a better future for yourself.

Archangel Zadkiel supports those born under the Gemini sign, who, like their patron angel, are great at learning and teaching. Like their angel, most often, you will find Geminis involved in mental pursuits such as research and study. In fact, regardless of your zodiac, you should seek Zadkiel's help for organized study and improved exam results.

Archangel Zadkiel appears in a deep, purplish blue light; his gemstone is lapis lazuli. Seek his help if you want to recall or remember things you have forgotten.

Cancer

Those born between June 22 and July 23 are Cancerians and are governed by Archangel Gabriel, an important archangel who has already been discussed in the section above. Pray to him for strength, and he will deliver.

Cancerians love staying at home. They are nurturing, caring, sensitive, and protective about their homes. Like their patron angel, they are excellent but strict parents who take parenthood seriously. Like Archangel Gabriel, Cancerians are extremely family-oriented.

Leo

People born between July 24 and August 23 fall under the Leo zodiac sign, ruled over by Archangel Raziel, the keeper of mysteries and secrets. Raziel is tasked with being the gatekeeper of supreme knowledge and divine mysteries. He guides each soul to its destiny, helping each soul rise up to meet and merge with the divine because he knows the purpose and the hidden capabilities of each soul.

He is the angel to call upon if you need to disengage confusing and indecipherable thoughts, ideas, and dreams. He will help you sort out these thoughts so that you can move forward. He is the one to seek to deepen your faith because he can reveal all hidden mysteries and truths. Archangel Raziel appears in a rainbow-colored light.

With his rainbow-colored aura, Archangel Raziel is a perfect match for Leo, ruled by the sun, because there is no rainbow without the sun. And without the rainbow, life would be boring. The Leo sign is all about drama and being showy. Like the rainbow, people born under this sign are often the center of attraction.

Virgo

People born between August 24 and September 23 are Virgos, and their guardian angel is Archangel Metatron, the owner and user of the Merkabah, the powerful energy tool shaped from Platonic solids. He uses the Merkabah to clear the lower, negative energies in the world and also to heal. The Virgo sign has a strong connection to healing as well. Like their patron angel, people born under the Virgo sign love to help and serve others through their healing powers.

Call upon Archangel Metatron when your energy is unbalanced and blocked. He will spin his magical Merkabah cube to clear your energy and lift your spirits. Archangel Metatron and Archangel Sandalphon are the only two angels who were once human beings.

In his human birth, Archangel Metatron was Enoch, the one who authored the book on esoteric knowledge, "The Book of Enoch." Archangel Metatron is the "scribe of gods" and a teacher of esoteric teachings. Further, he is the angel to turn to if you are a beginner in the world of spirituality. He will guide you to take baby steps and steady yourself before you dive deep into spirituality.

Libra

Those whose birthdays fall between September 24 and October 23 are Librans and are governed by Archangel Jophiel, the angel of beauty.

Like its patron angel, Libra is associated with Venus, who is personified as Aphrodite, the goddess of love and beauty.

Both Archangel Jophiel and the Librans take balance and harmony very seriously. Archangel Jophiel helps restore balance and harmony in any dissonant, conflicting environment. Call upon him when you want to clear your life of unwanted, negative, and havoc-wreaking thoughts and feelings.

Jophiel is also known as the "feng-shui" angel, the one who wants to rearrange your thoughts to create beauty and love. The patron angel of Librans reminds them that beautiful thoughts and feelings bring beauty and love into their lives. Negative thoughts create chaos and problems.

If you want help with your speech, seek his counsel. If you want to uplift yourself spiritually or for self-motivation, Archangel Jophiel is the one to turn to. If you want a relaxing and peaceful environment, call upon this angel of peace and harmony whose energy color is yellow and whose crystal is citrine.

Scorpio

People born between October 24 and November 22 fall under the zodiac sign Scorpio, which is ruled over by Archangel Jeremiel, whose name means "*mercy of God.*" He is the angel of emotional problems and helps you deal with your emotions.

His primary function is to guide the souls of recently dead people so that they may seek God's mercy and help them learn and review the lessons life has taught them. He doesn't just deal with dead people. Archangel Jeremiel helps the living to review and relearn lessons from their past mistakes so that they can create better tomorrows.

Call upon Jeremiel when you or someone you know is facing the fear of death. He teaches and shows you that God has better plans for you and that you have to face all fears, including fear of death, because the afterlife is waiting to welcome you. Seek his help to overcome feelings of bitterness and betrayal so that you can learn to build trust again.

Archangel Jeremiel is the perfect angel for Scorpios because this sign guides profound topics like death, grief, pain, and rebirth. People born under this zodiac sign are the deepest-thinking people and often do not hesitate to access the darkest corners of their souls to learn from and clear them of all negativities.

Sagittarius

People born between November 23 and December 22 are Sagittarians who are ruled over by Archangel Raguel, the *"friend of God."* He represents social order, family, and relationships.

His primary function is to heal conflicts, misunderstandings, and arguments so that peace and harmony reign. If you need quarrels resolved or ended, then you should seek Raguel's help. He comes to mediate arguments and helps to find solutions even in disagreements. He helps to enhance cooperation among group and family members.

Also known as the *"angel of fairness,"* he eliminates discrimination and harassment resulting in peace and harmony in the social order. If you feel you are not getting respect for what you do and your position, then you should seek his protection to set your situation right. His symbol is a judge's gavel, and his energy color is white or pale blue.

Like their patron angel, Sagittarians are also driven by the desire to set wrongs right in the world, including poverty, discrimination, lack of human rights, etc. Turn to your archangel and seek his help to achieve your desire. He is perfectly compatible with your drive.

Capricorn

People born between December 23 and January 20 fall under the zodiac sign of Capricorn, ruled over by Archangel Azrael. Called the *"angel of death,"* Azrael helps the souls of deceased people cross over to the other side and helps the grieving survivors deal with the loss of their loved ones. He also helps dead people see their entire life unfolding before them. If you are struggling with the grief of losing someone, seek Archangel Azrael's help and counsel.

Archangel Azrael is perfect for Capricorn because it is believed and known that even as children, people born under this sign exude wisdom way beyond their years. There's an old saying that *"Capricorns are born old."* Further, like their patron angel, Capricorns are fascinated by death and the afterlife. They are not afraid of death but are just curious and fascinated by mortality.

The acceptance of mortality is why Capricorns work so hard in their lives. They know their time is limited here and, therefore, feel driven to finish all the work they need to before their time comes.

Aquarius

People born between January 21 and February 19 are Aquarians governed by Archangel Uriel, one of the four primary angels who have already been discussed earlier in this chapter. Uriel is the most cerebral of all archangels, and therefore, his pairing with Aquarians is perfect. People born under this air sign are known to live in their heads and rarely depend on what their heart is saying.

People born under the Aquarius sign continuously think, leading to innovations and inspired ideas. This relentless thinking makes them highly intellectual too. They are detached, allowing them to view life objectively and make sensible decisions. Archangel Uriel is also known as the "intellectual angel."

Pisces

People born between February 20 and March 20 are the Pisceans ruled over by Archangel Sandalphon, the "Brother" who is tasked with delivering the messages and prayers of human beings to God, working along with Archangel Metatron. He helps to connect with your intuition. He is also connected with sounds and music and often makes his presence felt through your favorite song or music. Like Sandalphon, Pisces is also associated with music and songs.

Pisces is connected with water, and Archangel Sandalphon is connected with peace; therefore, they are made for each other. In the cycle of zodiac signs, Pisces is the most senior. He has seen the entire life cycle before him and is ready to step into the higher realms of consciousness. Pisces is the sign that is happy to return home to Heaven just as its patron angel is ever ready to take messages and prayers to Heaven.

To end this chapter and this section, it is important to note that although each astrological zodiac sign has dedicated archangels, there are no boundaries or restrictions among the divine creations. You can call upon or access the power and sacredness of any of the 12 archangels to help you, and they will heed your call because He commands them to do so.

Chapter Five: Finding Your Spirit Guide

Angels and archangels are both often referred to as "spirit guides." But spirit guides can be lots of other things as well. This chapter explores various other types of spirit guides that are out there, and you can seek their help and counsel.

So, how do you define *"spirit guide?"* There are many definitions depending on your culture. For example, Africans believe that ancestors become eternal spirits with a passionate interest in the lives of their living descendants. These ancestor guides are on a superior level as compared to living people.

They could be dead parents, grandparents, great-grandparents, and family members (even those who came before them!) The Africans believe that the spirits of dead people form a bridge between the living and the Almighty. The people belonging to ancient African tribes continue to revere their dead ancestors through regular rituals and communicate and interact with them for their help and wise counsel.

The spirits of dead people are believed to form a bridge between the living and the invisible in Africa.
https://unsplash.com/photos/HfGEtmnRwuE?utm_source=unsplash&utm_medium=referral&utm_content=creditShareLink

According to Native Americans, spirit guides live in the spiritual world and appear when you call them. Like guardian angels, these spirit guides take note of their wards right from their childhood and stay with them until their last day on Earth, giving them advice and counsel whenever needed. Spirit guides make themselves known to their wards through dreams, visions, music, etc. According to Western spiritualism, a spirit guide is a spiritual being who guides and protects a living person.

Everyone has spirit guides regardless of the religion they follow or the culture they come from. Spirit guides work for everyone, helping people during difficult times, warning them of impending challenges, and guiding them in their daily lives. They are around, always. They can come in different forms and serve different purposes. But they are there for you, to comfort you, and let you know you are alone.

Types of Spirit Guides

Spirit guides come in different forms and shapes, as mentioned above. They could come in the form of a gust of wind that gives you gooseflesh. They could come in the form of animals and plants, gods and goddesses, and even inanimate objects. After all, all things in this cosmos are interconnected and come from the same source, the ultimate divine will.

Trans-Species Spirits Guides

Often, spirit guides manifest themselves in two or more combinations of species. For example, spirit guides can be half-human and half-animal. The animal part could be a wolf, lion, horse, etc. For example, mermaids, half-woman and half-fish; fauns, half-human and half-goat; sphinx, half-human and half-lion; harpies, half-woman and half-bird, etc.

Many trans-species deities in different cultures are also worshiped as spirit guides. For example, Lord Ganesha, the elephant-head god in Hinduism; Anubis, the jackal-headed Egyptian god; Ra, the falcon-head Egyptian god, etc. Most importantly, your spirit guide manifests himself in the form you want to see.

Ancestors as Spirit Guides

Your ancestors, who have a connection through your blood, often come as spirit guides to help you. An ancestral guide could be a deceased relative's spirit, including parents, grandparents, great-grandparents, and even those before them.

Shamans often connect with the ancestors of seekers during shamanic journeys to help them unravel mysteries of the past, the effects of which affect the living. These ancestor spirit guides can lift old curses and heal old illnesses carried forth in the genetic materials of their families so that the present generation is free from those curses and issues. You can also connect with your ancestral guides for their help and counsel.

Spirit Guides as Totems and Animals

Animals are common spirit guides in multiple cultures. Shamans who travel across different planes of consciousness usually have an animal guide to guide them in the world of spirits, ensuring their safety while they are there and making sure they return to the human world unharmed.

Also called spirit animals, these spirit guides have the power and energy of the animal they come from. Native Americans believe that jaguars are ancestors who walk the world of the living as spirit guides. Wolves are commonly seen as spirit guides. Although there is no restriction on the animal that a spirit guide likes to take the shape of, jaguars, wolves, bears, etc., are often believed to be used by them.

Also, spirit animals need not be something as exotic as a jaguar or any other wild animal. It could be a loving pet who has passed on. They can also be your spirit guides. Alternatively, you could be drawn to a dancing peacock in a zoo or a wildlife safari. It could be a deer that appears in your dreams.

Gods and Goddesses as Spirit Guides

Gods and goddesses have been worshiped, and continue to be worshiped, in almost every religion and culture of the world. Multiple male and female deities are spirit guides. Some of them include Lord Ganesh, Athena, Apollo, Kali, Lakshmi, Shiva, Horus, Krishna, and there are many, many more. An entire chapter is dedicated to gods and goddesses later in this book.

Plants as Spirit Guides

Shamans have plant guides as well. The most common psychoactive plant in Shamanism is Ayahuasca, a common vine in Peru. Interestingly, Ayahuasca is known as the *"vine of the soul."* Experienced and wise shamans consume Ayahuasca and feel guided by the plant's spirit to the place where they can find answers to questions they seek, either for themselves or other seekers who come to them for help. Other plants that are taken as spirit guides include San Pedro, a species of cacti, and others.

In addition to psychoactive plants being spirit guides, even normal plants and trees can be your spirit guides, especially those that carry memories for you. Certain plants, flowers, fruit, etc., tend to stimulate your brain toward emotional and mental expansions. These plants are also spirit guides.

Ascended Masters

These masters once lived on Earth and have moved on to the higher realms, either after death or through spiritual awakening. They don't die, nor are they reborn. Their spirits hover around, just waiting for your call so that they can come to your aid. These ascended masters signify the ultimate teachers (called "gurus" in Sanskrit). They are not teachers who teach subjects; they are mentors who help you lead a better life and uplift your soul toward the divine.

Examples of ascended masters include Jesus, Mother Mary, Lord Buddha, Confucius, Kuthumi, and many more. You can find ascended masters in your own culture and religion.

How to Connect with and Summon Your Spirit Guide

Ask

The first step to connecting with your spirit guide is *to ask*. Get into the habit of asking your spirit guide for help. Your spirit guide(s) are always with you and around you. And they may even know that you need help. Yet, the seeker always has to take the first step. The giver usually waits for the request and then gives wholeheartedly. The more you seek, the more connected you will be with your spirit guide.

Ask specifically, not generally. To do this, you must have a list of your needs and desires. This is a seemingly silly but important thing to do too. You need to be very clear about what you seek. What kind of help are you looking for? Be specific with your requests. Only then can the spirit guide respond with specific messages.

For example, don't just say, *"Give me success in my career."* Instead, ask for specific things in your career, such as, *"Give me a promotion (mention the next rank that you seek) so that my income improves."* Don't just say, *"Give me happiness."* Instead, ask how you want happiness to be manifested in your life. For example, *"I would be happy if I could get [mention the person's name] to fall in love with me."*

Seek help specifically and ask for signs from your spirit guide that they have heard you. Once you get the signs, give thanks before you close the session. The gratitude message should also be as if you have already received what you sought. For example:

- "Thank you, my dear spirit guide, for giving me the solutions to my issues in my relationships."
- "Thank you, my dear spirit guide, for showing me how to improve myself to get that promotion I seek."
- "Thank you, my dear spirit guide, for helping me find my soulmate."

Seek Help from the Right Spirit Guides

Seek the guides of the highest truth. This is a critical aspect of summoning spirit guides. Like the human world, the spirit world is inhabited by all kinds of spirits – the good, the bad, and the ugly. This isn't about physical profiles but energy profiles. So, you must call upon the good, kind, and compassionate spirits and keep away from the harmful ones.

Ensure you are psychically protected before summoning spirit guides to prevent the wrong ones from causing you harm. Here are some tips for psychic protection:

Your summoning ritual should ideally take place in your sacred space, discussed in detail in an earlier chapter of this book.

- **First, ground yourself.** There are different ways to do this. Take a bath before the ritual so that your body feels clean and ready.
- **Smudge your sacred space.** Light up one end of a smudge stick (usually made of Sage or Palo Santo) to do this. Wave your hand all over the sacred space, ensuring every nook and cranny gets a waft of smoke from the smudge stick. This method will dispel and keep negative energy out of your sacred space.
- **Meditate for a few minutes** before the ritual to completely calm down and relax. Connect your body to the earth as you sit down for the ritual. Visualize a powerful ray of brown light securing you at your root chakra.

Scrying

Scrying is an ancient tool used for divination and to connect with the spirit world. A crystal ball, a mirror, smoke, or a clear surface of the liquid is used for scrying. People whose visual sense is powerful use scrying to connect with their spirit guides.

Dream Work

Here are some tips for using dreams to contact your spirit guide. Before going to bed, set an intention to meet your spirit guide in your dream.

- Keep a pen and paper near your bed so that you can make notes of your dreams as soon as you get up while it is still fresh in your mind. Create a dream journal recording your dreams and the experiences you had.
- What you need to find is repetitive patterns in your dreams. Re-read the chapter on how guardian angels can communicate with you. Use the lessons in that chapter to find repetitive patterns of numbers, words, symbols, or anything else that stands out in your dreams.

- Relive your dream. If the dream happened in a familiar setting, visit that place and do what you were doing in your dream. For example, if you were walking down a familiar street, take a walk down that street as you did in your dream. You will be amazed at the number of insights you will get from transferring your dream into a real experience.
- Tarot cards. Use your tarot cards to decipher what your spirit guide is telling you. For example, set the intention of understanding your dream and deciphering the message of your spirit guides. Then pull out the cards, place them in one of the many tarot card layouts, and try to interpret the messages the cards give you.

Do this for two weeks, and you will find a pattern emerging from your dreams. Depending on what you sought from your spirit guides, you will likely find your spirit guide's counsel or answer in these patterns.

Experiencing the Presence of and Signs of Spirit Guides

People experience the presence of spirit guides in different ways, including:

Through your inner knowledge: You may just feel or sense your spirit guide's presence. You could "hear" a voice that is audible only to you. The presence is unmistakable even if they are not tangible. Your inner self and/or your instincts simply know they are present.

Light sparks: You suddenly see sparks of light in front of your eyes. These sparks are clear indicators of the presence of your spirit guide.

Free-falling books: Sometimes, they just push a book from the shelf to grab your attention. The book itself could be a message or just to awaken your intuition so that you can read the signs they are sending you.

Free writing: Sometimes, you may feel compelled to pick up a pen and notebook and write something. This could be a way for your spirit guides to send you a message. Don't force yourself to write anything. Just place the pen on the paper and do free writing; just words and phrases are enough to make you understand. Spirit guides do not care about grammar and spelling; they just want you to experience their presence and pass on key messages to you.

Bibliomancy: This is the practice of opening a book (often a spiritual book like the Bible, the Torah, the Gita, the Quran, or any other book that you intuitively pick) and reading a random passage or line from it. Remember, you are doing all this intuitively, which is the way to communicate with spirit guides.

Here are some more important points to remember while you are communicating with your spirit guide:

- **Be fully present**, ensuring you are completely aware and conscious of your surroundings. Being present also includes being aware of the energy within the surroundings. What kind of energy are you radiating into the environment? What kind of energy are you experiencing from the environment? Do you have expectations? Get rid of them. Just do what the present moment is telling you. Feel and be natural.
- **Listen well.** Signs from your spirit guides can also come in the form of sounds. Meditation helps quieten your mind so that you can hear the subtle voices and sounds of your spirit guide as he or she speaks to you. Meditation also helps to slow your energy vibration down to align with the energy vibration of the spiritual world, which makes it easy to connect with your spirit guide.
- **Develop regular spiritual practices.** Spirit beings are not of this world. Therefore, you need to have regular spiritual practices to stay connected with them. They could be simple practices, nothing elaborate. For example, you could draw a tarot card every morning to understand what the day holds for you. Meditate for 10 minutes to enhance your connection with your higher self, the one who has direct access to the spirit world. Attend spiritual gatherings where you meet people who are more experienced than you and who can teach you the way of the spirit world. Learn to use different divination tools, including tarot cards, scrying, oracles, cards, etc.

This chapter ends by discussing gratitude, one of the most important elements of connecting with your spirit guide. Your connection with your spirit guide should always be from a place of gratitude instead of from a place of neediness. The more you are grateful, the more service and love you will get from your spirit guides. They don't need to be paid with money or riches; they want to be included in your life because they are here for you. Acknowledging their presence is the first step toward being grateful. Show them you are grateful for their guidance and love.

Don't say, *"Why haven't you given me what I want?"* Instead, say, *"I am grateful for your presence in my life. Thank you for lighting up my life with your presence. Thank you for offering me solutions and counsel."* When you question their help, there is distrust. When you embrace their offerings, there is trust.

Chapter Six: Following Your Animal Guide

Strictly speaking, an animal guide is not a guardian. Instead, it guides you toward the answers to the questions you ask. Animal guides are usually found in shamanic and astral journeys. In many cultures, animal spirits are spiritual guides who present themselves to help navigate difficult patches in your life. In shamanic journeys, they guide and protect the shamans as they walk through the world of the spirits seeking answers to various questions.

Animals can also be spirit guides.
https://pixabay.com/images/id-1836875/

How to Find Your Animal Guide

As you experience the appearance of your spirit animal, as a beginner, you may find it weird, scary, or even bizarre. Reilly, a novice in spirit world experiences, took time to overcome his fear and uncertainty. He kept dreaming of wolves in the wild and got caught amidst a pack. However, the fear soon turned to something pleasant when he noticed, with each successive dream, that he could get closer to the animals, and one wolf specifically.

With every dream he had, the one that seemed to be drawn to him as he was to it, kept coming closer until one night, he was able to reach out and touch it without fear. The other wolves simply vanished that day. The wolf spoke to him and told him to free himself from the shackles that were holding him back. The wolf, who called herself Rexi, counseled him to use his intelligence and wisdom and live the life he was meant to. So, in this case, the animal guide came in Reilly's dreams. Here are some other ways you can find your spirit animals.

Learn about animal connections in your lineage or culture. Avoid following animal guides simply because they appear more exotic. It cannot really be your animal guide if you don't feel connected to an animal.

For example, for Native Americans, jaguars and wolves often appear as animal guides. However, if you are not a Native American, it is highly unlikely that you will feel a connection to these animals. Do some research within your lineage and find out which animal has a strong connection to your family. Often, this animal will be your animal guide too.

Pay attention to your dreams to see if any animal has repeatedly made an appearance there. Make entries in your dream journal. If you already have a dream journal, look back at your earlier records and see if you have made notes of animal appearances. Otherwise, notice them in your present dreams and make notes. Animal guides often present themselves in your dreams.

Recall your past experiences with animals. Did you have a favorite pet that died, and you missed it so much that you haven't got another pet since? If yes, is this pet appearing in your visions, dreams, or thoughts? It doesn't have to be pets. It could be a chance encounter in the wild while you visit a family or friend in a remote area. Or you suddenly came face to face with an animal while traveling, and you felt an unmistakable connection with this animal.

Ask yourself if you feel drawn to any animal. Meditate on this question. Sit in a quiet, undisturbed place and close your eyes. After your body and mind fully relax, let your intuition guide you to any animal you feel drawn to. Ask yourself what this animal is trying to teach you. If your thought moves to another animal, then move on. Ask the same question to yourself. What is this animal trying to teach you, especially in connection with your spiritual journey and building your inner strength?

Repeat this exercise for as many animals as you want to. Make detailed notes of your intuitive conversations with yourself on each animal. Do this exercise for about a week. Forget about this exercise for a few days and return to your journal after that. See which animal resonates with you the most and what lessons it may be trying to teach you. This animal could be your animal guide.

Some people may find their animal guide quickly, while others could take some time to do so. There is nothing right or wrong about it. The most important thing is to find your animal guide, the one that your heart, mind, and spirit resonate with in perfect harmony. Remember, your animal guide is looking for you as much as you seek it. When the time comes, you will both find each other. Relax, be kind to yourself, and continue your search.

Common Animals as Animal Guides

Here is a list of common animals and their spiritual significance to help you understand how animals can be your guide in the spiritual world.

Bear - The bear is a deeply emotional animal and has a strong connection with the outdoors. The bear stands for courage, strength, and determination. They don't give up, and they don't forget. If your animal guide is a bear or if you feel drawn to a bear, it is likely that you are a natural, strong-willed leader. It also means you have little or no patience with people who cannot keep up with you and, therefore, end up being independent (or lonely, depending on your outlook on life).

Butterfly - The butterfly is an iconic symbol of transformation and new beginnings as it develops into a beautiful butterfly from its struggles as a larva trapped in a cocoon and then as a "creepy" caterpillar doing nothing but eating for days on end. The butterfly demonstrates that everyone will have their day on Earth. You just need to persist, persevere, and work patiently and diligently toward that day when you can break free and soar. If the butterfly is your spirit animal, you will likely be highly adaptable and open to changes and new experiences.

Beaver - The beaver is a hardworking, determined creature associated with family and community. It is known for its uncanny ability to persevere through tough times. If your spirit animal is a beaver, then it is likely that you are also a hardworking, determined person with a lot of stamina and a good head for problem-solving.

Cat - Great instincts, curiosity, and adventure form the core of a cat's personality, not to mention independence and self-confidence. Cats are also the epitome of patience. If your animal guide is a cat, then it is likely that you are also a highly independent, intuitive person and have a powerful sense of self.

Cheetah - The cheetah signifies agility and grace. It is a master of camouflage, and in some cultures, it is a patron of hunters and warriors. If you are drawn to cheetahs, you will likely have a career in athletics or any other performing arts that call for speed and/or grace. The cheetah reminds you never to stop exploring both the external and internal worlds.

Deer - The deer signifies innocence, kindness, and gentleness. Deer are intelligent animals known for their grace. If your spirit animal is a deer, you will likely be kind, intelligent, and considerate. Deers strike a graceful balance between success and gentleness. Personal integrity is paramount for you, both from yourself and others around you, with a deep connection to nature.

Dove - The dove, a bird of optimism and hope, stands for peace and blessings. Doves also represent new beginnings. Doves are gentle and understanding animal guides. They remind you to spread your positivity and embrace tranquility and peace. They can guide you to your soulmate and teach you to cherish your loved ones.

Dolphin - Dolphins are social, playful, and friendly animals. If your animal guide is a dolphin, it is likely that you are also a highly social and friendly person who is ever ready to have a good time. People drawn to dolphins are also known to read people and understand their feelings, just like dolphins, who are very intelligent and compassionate.

Eagle - Eagles stand for vision, freedom, and bravery. If your spirit animal is an eagle, you are also likely to be free-spirited with a strong sense of self and a clear vision for your life.

Elephant - The elephant stands for spiritual understanding, wisdom, determination, and gentleness despite its huge size and strong body and will. It is also known for its intelligence and loyalty. If your spirit animal is an elephant, you could also be an intelligent, strong-willed, and determined individual, along with being a loyal friend who puts others' needs ahead of your own. People who identify with elephants as their animal guides tend to have a powerful sense of power and strength.

Frog - Surprisingly, frogs are popular animal guides, despite their seeming sliminess. They heal emotional and physical wounds. They remind people to check in with themselves, dig up their past trauma, face it, heal themselves, and move on to a better tomorrow. Frogs teach you the uselessness of living in the past and the importance and significance of living in the present.

Fox - The fox is a master of camouflage and detachment. He adapts very well, harnessing the power of his surroundings with his cleverness which some people like to refer to as "sly." Cunning is the middle name of foxes, as they are adept at turning any situation to their advantage. In many cultures, foxes are guides who help people who are lost find their way back. If you find kinship with a fox, then it is likely that you are an artist, writer, or any other creative person.

Horse - The horse stands for passion and drive. Connecting with a horse could make you a highly goal-oriented individual. This majestic animal signifies freedom and endurance too.

Hawk - The hawk is a highly perceptive bird with the capability to see things from all sides. It is also connected with compassion and empathy. The hawk teaches you that you can let your imagination soar even as you keep your hold on reality. People who have hawks as their animal guides are believed to have a deeper and easier connection with the spirit world than others.

Jaguar - The jaguar is a symbol of courage, protection, and temerity. It is associated with decisiveness and powerful intuition. The appearance of this spirit animal is a message from the divine world that you must trust your instincts. If your spirit animal is a jaguar, it is likely that you are always ready for change.

Lion - The lion, the king of beasts, represents courage, strength, and royalty with a natural sense of leadership and authority. People with a lion as their animal guide tend to have careers in leadership roles or study history and/or mythology.

Mouse - The mouse signifies the importance of scrutiny and detail, reminding you not to overlook the seemingly trivial aspects of your life.

Owl - An owl can see what others miss. They go beyond the surface of things, dig deep into everything, and discover hidden treasures. People who have owls as their animal guides tend to be wiser beyond their ears. Such people are referred to as "old souls." The owl also signifies rebirth. They remind you that death is only a side effect of life, a renewal, not the end. If you feel stuck in a rut, the sight of an owl might indicate a time for transition and change.

Peacock - The peacock is a bird of reinvention and awakening. The peacock reminds you that it is never too late for positive change. You could be highly creative and resourceful if you have a peacock as your spirit animal. You have the ability to find innovative solutions to problems.

Possum – A possum stands for resilience and adaptability. You know that possums play dead to escape being killed by their prey. This amazing ability to survive is the reason they are known for their adaptability and resilience. This animal teaches you that playing dead to survive is a useful lesson to learn and master. Since it is a nocturnal creature, possums can help you tap into the darkest corners of your mind so that you swim against the tide and come ashore safe and sound.

Turtle - The hallmarks of a turtle are endurance, patience, and wisdom. If you feel drawn to turtles, it could likely mean that you are determined and patient and value wisdom over cleverness or materialistic intelligence. Also, the turtle teaches you to go slow and steady in life, and this lesson works really well when you feel stuck in a rut. Just remind yourself to take one little step at a time, and soon your goal will be near. The turtle also represents your inward journey toward peace and understanding.

Tiger - Tiger is the epitome of courage and strength. The tiger can easily guide you through your difficult times by helping you find your inner power and strength. If your animal spirit is a tiger, you tend to catch on to some of its confidence and majestic power. You find the strength to continue working with added vim and vigor and the courage to face all challenges fearlessly.

Wolf - The wolf represents freedom, intuition, and intelligence. The wolf reminds you not to forget your primal instincts because they are the oldest of your abilities. Wolves are associated with awareness, family, and communication. So, suppose you are drawn to a wolf. In that case, you are likely to be a family-oriented person who values relationships and friendships. You could also be a great communicator with a wolf as your animal guide.

Working with Your Spirit Animal

Once you have found your animal guide, be open to learning the lesson it is trying to teach you. Here are some tips which will help you:

Find out the symbolic meaning of your spirit animal. Re-read the above section dealing with common animal guides and their spiritual meaning. If your animal guide is not on that list, do some research and gather information regarding the animal and what it stands for: its strengths, weaknesses, and way of life. The more you learn about your guide, the better you will understand its connection to you and the lessons it is trying to teach you.

Do not humanize your animal guide. If you try to deal with your spirit animal the way you would with a human relation or friend, it will silence its unique way of communicating with you and expressing itself. Instead, open your heart and mind and be receptive to their way of expression and communication. Embracing their way of life is the way forward for you. Don't force humanity's way of life on them.

Apply these lessons from your guide's way of life in your life. For example, before taking an important decision, take a step back, and ask yourself how your animal guide would react in this situation. What would be your guide's decision? Talk to your spirit animal and seek advice and counsel. It will send you a message. Follow its advice and let it guide you to the right decision.

Further, think about three important life goals that could be connected with your animal guide; short-term, medium-term, and long-term goals. Apply your animal guide's lessons to these goals and work toward them as your guide would.

Pay attention to the experiences that involve your spirit animal. Whenever you see anything that connects you to your spirit animal, stop for a while and register the experience. You could come across the animal in a poem, book, movie, poster, random conversation, etc. Be aware of these situations and try to understand what your animal guide is trying to convey to you. Whenever you notice these things, ask yourself these questions:

- What are your feelings when you see your spirit animal? Do you feel a sense of foreboding or a sense of joy?
- Is your spirit animal trying to lead you in any particular direction? To do this, notice the way the animal's head is turned or anything else that could convey this meaning.
- Are you at a crossroads in your life? Have you sought help from the spirit world? If yes, what is the help you need? Can the appearance of your spirit animal be the answer to what you seek?

Honor your spirit animal. The more you honor and venerate its presence in your life, the deeper the bond will be. You can place idols of your spirit animal in your home or sacred space. You can wear symbols representing your spirit animal. Most importantly, give gratitude as often as you can.

The last and most important tip about finding and connecting with your animal guide is that you must do what resonates with you the most. Also, some people have one spirit animal right throughout their lives. However, this condition is not mandatory. Many shamans and other healers have more than one spirit animal in their repository.

The one that appears at a particular time is aligned with the specific need of that time. Quite often, a spirit animal may appear just once in a lifetime, help you in one situation, and never come back. The spirit world is dynamic and can change shape and form depending on your needs. So, don't worry if your animal guide changes. It is a perfectly valid thing to happen.

Chapter Seven: Calling Upon Ancestors and Departed Loved Ones

As you already know, spirit guides come in different forms. This chapter focuses on departed loved ones, family members, and ancestors who can come as spirit guides in your life. In almost all cultures around the world, family members and loved ones who die automatically become ancestors.

The spirits of your dead relatives find a home in the world of ancestors, and they meet the spirits of other relatives who died before them. The spirits of your ancestors continue to look down on you and can become your guides if you are willing to accept their presence and listen to their advice.

The spirit of your loved ones who have passed away continue to watch over you.
https://pixabay.com/images/id-3777403/

When loved ones pass on, they don't eat at the table, come to the movies with you, play, and laugh with you. You cannot hug them and feel their beating hearts. They don't hold your hand or pat your back. They are not in the form that you knew them when they were living. And yet, they are there, always by our side, waiting to help you in your need.

In many cultures, praying to departed souls is a regular ritual at least once a year. Freshly cooked food is placed on the table for the ancestors. Ancestor spirits are invited for the meal. A few minutes are given for the spirits to sit at the table and taste the food that is served before the living family members partake in the same food.

You can also call upon the spirits of your loved ones and ancestors to seek their guidance and advice. They will become your spirit guides if you ask them.

Connecting with Your Ancestors

Everyone can connect with ancestors and departed loved ones. This ability is not restricted only to the "psychically gifted" people because people are all innately gifted in this regard. In fact, you are likely to have had instances before in your life where the spirits of your ancestors and departed loved ones have spoken to you. Here are a few examples of when the spirit of someone you loved tried to communicate with you. You may likely have brushed it off as a coincidence or something else:

- You may have experienced something strange like a warning before you heard about the sudden death of a loved one or friend
- You may have observed a sign connected with the deceased at his or her funeral
- You may have seen your loved ones in your dream with a specific message you couldn't fathom
- You may have heard the voice of your departed loved ones, which you thought was in your head
- You may have seen something in a faraway location bearing an uncanny resemblance connected with a departed loved one

All these could have been signs from the spirit of the dead person. Because you did not know or were not aware that the spirits of departed loved ones can talk to you, you did not pay attention to these signs. Now that you know, keep your body, mind, and heart open to receiving messages from your loved ones who have moved on from the physical world. Here are some recommendations on how to connect with the spirit of your loved ones:

Create a sacred ritual - Many cultures have detailed rituals to connect with their ancestors regularly. In Hinduism, there are specific days in a year and month called "pitr days" where offerings are made to the ancestors. "Pitr" means ancestors in Sanskrit. In many cultures, offerings are made on the death date, birth date, or other special occasions in honor of ancestors. Here are a few more examples of dedicated ancestor worship from around the world:

- In ancient Mexican and Spanish culture, people worship their ancestors on the "Day of the Dead" or the "Día de Los Muertos" ceremony. They believe that the offerings made to their ancestors help them in their afterlife.

- Ancestor worship is common in the Vodun faith, and Vodun is commonly known as Voodoo in the West. However, there is much more to Voodoo than what is portrayed in popular culture. The people of the Vodun faith believe that the souls of the dead walk the living world on certain days, and it is their duty to honor them.

- In Chinese culture, the Shi ceremony, where a living person impersonates the dead person to whom the ritual is dedicated, is a common way to honor the spirits of ancestors.

- In Cambodia, Pchum Ben is a national holiday, and Pchum Ben is also called Ancestors' Day. On this day, every year, the Cambodians go back seven generations to honor and worship the spirits of their dead ancestors.

If your family already has such a ritual in place, make sure you participate in these ceremonies. Otherwise, you can create your own simple rituals. You could have a small altar with pictures of your departed family members. Lighting a candle for them is enough to let them know you are thinking of them.

Alternatively, you can donate to charity in their honor on their special days. Or simply gather all your family around, cook their favorite dishes, offer them food, and then eat and have a good time reminiscing about their days on earth. You could do this on special occasions or whenever you feel like connecting with them.

Talk to them as you connect with them. For example, as you light a candle in honor of a departed loved one, use their name and say what you want to tell them. Speak to them as if they are still alive and standing next to you. Visualize their response and respond accordingly. Or you can just say a few words of prayers to them.

Seek their help and try to work together on specific family issues. Write down the problem you are facing, and then see how you want to present the problem to your departed loved ones. Keep a pen and paper and write your question. Then wait for a while, and they will guide you to write down the answer to your question. Just be open to receiving their help. Meditation is also a great way to work with your ancestors. Sit quietly in an undisturbed place. Focus on the ancestor you want to call upon and meditate on them. They will make their presence felt and will answer your question too.

Knowing the Presence of Departed Loved Ones and Ancestors

How do departed loved ones make their presence known? Below are some clear signs that you should keep a look out for.

Their presence can be felt. There is a clearly discernible presence in your space. You might be alone in a room. But you know you are not alone. There is someone else there with you. It might be only a feeling. But the feeling is too real and strong to ignore. You can feel their emotions too. Be sensitive to this feeling and acknowledge it.

You can hear a voice. People with powerful auditory senses can hear the voice of their dear departed loved one. Claire lost her mother to cancer last year and is still struggling with the loss. Her mother was a huge pillar of support, and Claire couldn't get over her grief. She took a break from college, but that didn't help at all. In fact, having less to do deepened her grief and loneliness. She didn't have a father to lean on; he had left them a long time ago.

One day, as she lay alone, feeling desolate and lost, she heard her mother's voice, comforting, exhorting, and cajoling her to get on with her life. They had a long conversation where the mother-daughter duo recalled happy times they had experienced together. Her mother's final words were,

"My dear daughter, remember that I'm always by your side. I may not be visible to you as earlier. But I can see and feel you. You can also feel my presence. Reach out to me whenever you need me. But don't stop living your life. You deserve to move ahead and find happiness and love just as I did."

Claire was overcome with emotions after that conversation. But it helped her. She rejoined her college course and completed it with honors. She found a job of her liking, fell in love, got married, and had children. Her mother was always there, giving her help and advice whenever she needed it.

Sometimes, you can feel the touch of your departed loved one. You may feel their hug or embrace, or they may just pat you on the back. Even if this is rare, it happens, especially if you can recognize the touch of the departed person. For example, a wife can feel the hug of her departed husband. A child can feel the embrace of his or her mother.

Often, the spirit of your ancestor can communicate using a fragrance. For example, in the above example of Claire, her mother loved roses. Claire would smell roses even though no rose plants or flowers were nearby. It was her mother's way of telling her that she was close by. Claire would sense this fragrance when she sought her mother during stressful times.

Rarely may your departed loved one make themselves visible to you in their human form, fully or partially. The person could appear to you in their entire form, hale and hearty, and with a smile. Sometimes, you may see a hazy structure of their form. You tend to be most receptive to these images between the dreaming and waking states.

Sometimes, they use material forms to communicate with you. Lights might go off and on without reason. Books could fall off the shelves without anyone touching or moving them. The framed photo of the departed person may keep falling over. All these are ways of making their presence felt or getting your attention.

The spirits of departed loved ones may use symbols to communicate with you. Common symbols include rainbows, birds, flowers, butterflies, or other images that they loved during their lifetime. For example, if your spouse passed away recently and she or he loved butterflies, a butterfly could fly and land on your shoulder, signaling the presence of their spirit nearby.

Ancestor Veneration Ritual for Beginners

The ritual described in this section is specifically designed for beginners who are hoping to reconnect with lost ancestors. It could be that you are doing this for the first time or that your family, somewhere in the midst of modernization, has lost touch with the spirits of your ancestors.

The first thing you need to do before you start the ritual is to get the names of all your ancestors as far back as you can go. Speak to your living elderly relatives and find out the names of their grandparents and great-grandparents, who will all be your ancestors. Make notes of the names of your dead parents, grandparents, and great-grandparents. If someone in your family has a diary of a dead uncle or aunt, read it to learn more about your family. You could also include people who have cared for you during your childhood, including loving governesses, babysitters, home tutors, and others who have passed on.

Make sure you have fasted before the ritual for at least an hour. Next, light a white candle; just a simple candle you have at home will do. Place some unsliced bread and a glass of wine, or any other food that is loved by you and your family, in front of the candle. You can do this alone or include friends and family who want to be part of the ritual.

Settle down in your seat. Take a few deep breaths with your feet flat on the ground and relax. Then, say the following prayer:

> *"I remember my beloved ancestors and my parents (state the names if they have passed on, or use the last person who has passed on). I remember this is the food they ate. This is the place they lived and breathed. This is the wine they drank."*

At this point, read the names of all the ancestors which you have noted. After the name of every ancestor, say a short prayer for their soul, and thank the spirit for their presence in your life. Repeat the above prayer at the end of the list.

When you feel satisfied, tear a piece of the bread, take the wine glass in your hand, thank the spirits for the food and drink, and place it near the candle. Sit quietly for a while, giving the spirits time to take your offerings. After a few minutes, share the bread and wine with whoever is present in the ritual.

Before getting up, thank your ancestor spirits for coming, and give them permission to leave. Let the candle burn itself out. If you gaze long enough into the flame, you may see signs and visions in answer to the questions you seek. There are a number of ways that the spirits of departed loved ones could use to communicate and connect with you. You just need to open your heart and mind and allow the magical miracle to take place and impact your life positively. There is just one small point of discussion before ending this chapter. What is the difference between departed loved ones and ancestors?

Departed loved ones are those with whom you have had contact in your life. Your parents, grandparents, favorite uncles and aunts, cousins, siblings, even close friends, etc., are usually referred to as departed loved ones. Ancestors could go back many generations in your family from either of your parent's sides. They can also help you deal with problems.

Normally, the spirits of your old ancestors are called upon to solve pertinent family issues that have been in the family for years on end. Old ancestors from many generations ago are likely to have information to help you end the misery for future generations. So, you call upon your ancestors in this case. Nothing can stop these spirits from continuously being in your life after you have summoned them once and taken their help. They can become your best friends too.

The spirits of dear departed loved ones help you deal with your personal problems, like how Claire's mother helped her deal with her loss. So, call upon your favorite relative and take their help to improve your life or solve a persistent problem.

Chapter Eight: Connecting with Ascended Masters

Ascended Masters can also appear as one's spirit guide. Who are ascended masters? They are enlightened beings, the most evolved in the spiritual hierarchy. They are above even archangels and other spirit guides. They lived a life of the highest virtue, sacrificing all they had during their lifetime for the welfare of others and to realize the ultimate truth.

Examples of ascended masters are Buddha, Jesus, Moses, Melchizedek, Mary, St. Germaine, St. Francis, Yogananda, and many more. Connecting and communicating with ascended masters even once can be a life-changing encounter. While ascended masters can help you in various ways, their primary role in this universe is to help you increase your awareness of the spiritual energy that permeates everything in this world.

Buddha is of the ascended masters.
Nordwest, CC BY-SA 4.0 <https://creativecommons.org/licenses/by-sa/4.0>, via Wikimedia Commons https://commons.wikimedia.org/wiki/File:Buddha_in_Meditation_2023-05-11-22.jpg

Buddha's teachings were based on the fact that each person has the capability to reach Buddhahood – which means each one has the potential to become an ascended master. It is an innately human thing that lies buried deep in your psyche, covered by layers of desire and greed for materialism. The way to overcome these layers is achievable, even if difficult. You have to clear multiple obstacles and make positive but difficult life choices, and to do this relentlessly and long enough to achieve ascended mastership takes multiple rebirths.

The Making of Ascended Masters

Ascended masters themselves had to cross these hurdles and have had thousands of rebirths before achieving their hallowed status in their ultimate lifetime on this Earth. Every rebirth represents spiritual transformations they underwent to learn the deeper secrets of life so that they could ascend the spiritual plane and stay there for eternity, helping humankind. They use the process of self-mastery for spiritual transformation.

With every step of self-mastery, they become increasingly enlightened until they can willingly let go of their body and become a pure soul that ascends into the spiritual realm and becomes an ascended master. So, ascended masters are people like you – facing similar life challenges. What differentiates them from normal human beings is that they choose to express themselves as a pure reflection of Him or the divine will, sidelining baser human tendencies such as greed, desire, anger, fear, etc.

Becoming an ascended master is based on three crucial principles: karma, reincarnation, and ascension. Here, this chapter looks at these three elements in a bit more detail.

Karma - The concept of karma forms the core of Hinduism and Buddhism. But every religion, including Christianity, Judaism, Kabbalistic Jews, Islam, and others, speaks of this concept in some form or other. In the mainstream language of spirituality, karma can be translated as *"you reap what you sow,"* although the karmic concept runs deeper than that. Karma renders you accountable for every action you take and every choice you make.

According to the law of karma, what happens today in your life in the present moment is a result of your actions in the past which could be minutes, days, weeks, months, years, or lifetimes ago. Every "good" deed you do gives you "positive" points, and every "bad" deed gives you "negative" points. The reason for the quotation marks for the words good, bad, positive, and negative is that everything in this world is relative, and what is good today becomes bad tomorrow and vice versa. And thus, the karmic wheel continues.

The trick to increasing the chances of your ascension is to get off the karmic wheel. And the way to get off is to radiate compassion, kindness, and forgiveness at all times, regardless of what is happening with and around you. Ascended masters know that the answers to life's painful questions lie within you and not outside of you. So, whenever they faced challenges in their lives that brought out the negativity in them, they turned inward to face and deal with these negativities without allowing the poison to affect others around them.

These ascended masters dealt with their destructive desires similarly, ensuring no one got hurt. They dealt with their own negativities and used that energy to raise their vibrations for ultimate ascension. These masters know that everyone and everything in this world is interconnected, and negative aspects of life are the challenges and obstacles that help in self-mastery. No one, including yourself, needs to be blamed for anything. It is all the outcome of past actions, and the way off the karmic wheel is to deal with life compassionately and with kindness toward yourself and others around you.

Reincarnation - Karma makes you accountable, while reincarnation allows you to pay off your karmic debts, which, in turn, will help you get off the karmic wheel. Reincarnation or rebirth allows your soul to walk the path of evolution and progress toward enlightenment or ascension. The souls of the ascended masters are not compelled to take rebirth in the human world. They remain in the spiritual realm to teach, heal, and help human beings achieve higher vibrations.

Ascension - Ascension or enlightenment is nothing but the return of your soul to its divine origin. Everyone and everything in this universe has a divine spark that connects them to the ultimate divine or God. The ascension process involves opening your heart and mind to cut through the layers of baser instincts to reach your higher self and reconnect with that divine spark that lies embedded in your soul. Ascension and enlightenment include:

- Awakening of the mind by learning the lessons taught by the challenges and obstacles life throws at you.
- Awakening a new personality, thanks to the lessons learned through the awakening of the mind.
- Awakening of your spiritual energy, thanks to moving up from the baser instincts to higher realms of thinking and consciousness.

As you master the above steps, your soul will slowly but surely awaken until the final ascension and reunion with the ultimate divine.

Ascended Masters and Their Teachings

Buddha - Also known as the Enlightened One, Buddha was born as Prince Siddhartha into a royal family. At the time of his birth, wise sages predicted that he would either be an emperor of the world or a powerful ascetic. His father did not want him to be ascetic, so he made sure his son lived in luxurious comfort, hiding the sufferings and pain of the world from him.

But fate intervened, and Siddhartha left a life of luxury and went in search of the highest spiritual truth. When he found it after years of facing indeterminate obstacles and challenges, he became Buddha, the Enlightened One. He lives in the spiritual world, helping humanity lead a balanced life of "the middle path," a principle he proposed whereby moderation of everything is the key to happiness and reduced desire. He proposed the following four noble truths to achieve Buddhahood that is inherent in each one of us:

- Suffering is an innate aspect of existence
- Desire is the root of suffering
- Suffering can be ended by giving up desire
- And finally, Buddha proposed the eightfold path of how to give up desire. The eightfold path is composed of the following elements: right view, right thought, right speech, right action, right livelihood, right effort, right mindfulness, and right concentration.

Prayer to Buddha - *"Oh, Blessed Buddha, you are the vessel of compassion and bestower of peace. You love unconditionally and are the source of true happiness. Guide me to liberation and enlightenment."*

Babaji - Also known as Mahavatar Babaji or the deathless one, Babaji brought the ancient system of Kriya Yoga into mainstream life, helping thousands of people achieve balance, peace, and harmony in their lives. With his help, you can take yourself closer to the divine. He will guide you to follow God's will and His purpose for you in this lifetime. Babaji can assist you towards a clear commune with God, simplifying your life so that you are free to follow your spirituality, detaching yourself from excessive materialism, and reducing your desires and cravings from causing you harm.

Prayer to Babaji – *"Dear Babaji, I am grateful for your presence in my life. You are my guide and mentor, helping me through the muddling conflicts of life and teaching me ways to overcome the obstacles that stand in my path to reach you. I pray that you hold my hand and light my path during this life and the future life until my pure soul is freed from the karmic wheel."*

El Morya - El Morya was the son of the king of Kashmir, a beautiful kingdom in North India, who became a monk. He lived during the latter half of the 19th century, and he frequented the monasteries and retreats in the mighty Himalayas. He was one of the founding members of the Theosophical Society, established in 1875.

His previous births are believed to have been Abraham, Melchior (one of the three Magi), King Arthur, Thomas Becket, Sir Thomas More, and many more before he became an ascended master in his lifetime as El Morya. You can reach out to him when you need assistance in matters of faith, decision-making, psychic protection, and staying true to your principles and beliefs.

Prayer to El Morya – *"El Morya, you stand by my side at all times. In your name, I tread holy ground. You give me the strength to keep my days happy and holy in God's name. You and I are one. Keep me grounded and humble, and my heart and mind pointed toward Him alone."*

Jesus - Jesus is the one and only Son of God who was sent to earth by Him because of His deep, unfathomable love for humankind. Jesus felt the effects of temptations as ordinary men do. However, Jesus chose to rise above petty temptations and lead his followers to redemption and ascension. Call upon Jesus when you need clear communication with the divine in matters of forgiveness, steering clear of temptation, and healing of all kinds.

Prayer to Jesus – *"Dear Lord Jesus, open my ears so I can hear His word. Open my heart so I can embrace Him into my life. Open my mind so I can see His power. You are my pathway to Him. I beseech you never to abandon me."*

Kuthumi - Master Kuthumi (also spelled Koot Hoomi) lived many lives, including, but not limited to, Pythagoras, Balthazar (one of the three Magi), and St. Francis of Assisi. He was known as a master psychologist and was a big supporter of youth. He was one of the founding members of the Theosophical Society. He is the master you seek when you need to find your life purpose, problem-solving, and focus.

Prayer to Kuthumi – *"Dear Kuthumi, I beseech you to teach me through my own heart the truth I seek. Show me the answers I seek. Show me my life path and my purpose in this lifetime. Heal my physical and mental bodies so I may walk the path destined for me by Him."*

Moses - God called upon Prophet Moses to free the slaves from Egypt and lead them to the Promised Land. Upon God's command, he delivered the Ten Commandments to the Israelites. He is the master you should seek when experiencing diversity and needing a positive outlook. He promotes leadership qualities. Pray to Moses when you need the courage to face people in authority. Seek his help when your faith is shaken for any reason. He will work miracles for you.

Prayer to Moses – *"Dear glorious Moses, be my messenger to Him. Carry my message to Him. Ask Him to deliver me from my suffering. Teach me to stay grounded and faithful to Him and the path He laid for me. Work miracles for me so I may do His bidding in this life and hereafter."*

Melchizedek - His name translates to "king of righteousness." He was the priest of Salem and is mentioned in the Old Testament. He spoke of God being the "creator and deliverer." However, there is no record of his birth and death. He holds the masculine energy of the world, balancing the feminine energy of the Virgin Mary. Reach out to him to correct unpleasant circumstances, purification, psychic protection, and transformations.

Prayer to Melchizedek – *"Glorious St. Melchizedek, help me deal with the unpleasantness in my life bravely and without harm to anyone. Help me meditate on the prophecies you made and fill my life with purity so I may live the life He destined for me."*

St. Francis - St. Francis of Assisi is the patron saint of nature, especially the animal world. Born into a rich family, he served as a soldier and was a prisoner of war. During his time in jail, he received an epiphany from Jesus, exhorting him to set aside his worldly life and follow the spiritual path. Seek his help for your pet and animal needs, finding a career suited to your personality, spiritual devotion, and for your struggles against delinquency.

Prayer to St. Francis – *"Beloved St. Francis, teach me to love where there is hate. Teach me to forgive when I am hurt. Teach me to bring light when there is darkness. Teach me to stay strong in my faith and help me discover my true purpose."*

St. John – St. John is the patron of the sick and their caregivers. He is one of the 12 apostles of Jesus, the Son of God, who came to heal humanity and teach humans compassion and forgiveness. Seek the help of St. John when you are experiencing depression and anxiety. He heals heart ailments and helps you with spiritual dedication.

Prayer to St. John – *"St. John, heal my sickness. Teach me and my caregiver patience so we may pass this difficult phase with minimal difficulty. You are my patron and protector. Accept me as your student and show me the path to a disease-free life."*

Virgin Mary – Mother Mary became an ascended master many years before she took birth again to become the blessed vessel to carry Lord Jesus Christ. Before her birth as Virgin Mary, she lived the life of a nomad and left her tribe to live in a cave to spend her life in solitude and prayer. She became an ascended master in that life only. Seek her help when you need assistance regarding all matters of children, childbirth, and adoption. She is the mother of grace, faith, compassion, and mercy. She is a healer.

Prayer to Mother Mary – *"Dear Blessed Mother Mary, I beseech you to keep my children safe from all kinds of harm. Teach me compassion and kindness so I may transfer your lessons to my beloved children so they may transfer the knowledge to their children until the world is filled with compassionate and kind people, the world that He dreams of."*

Yogananda – Parahamsa Yogananda brought the world of Kriya Yoga from India to the Western world. He taught the Western world to meditate and chant so they may find inner peace and harmony and, in turn, reconnect with their soul. Call upon him to find peace, divine love, and all aspects of yoga that will free you from the burdens of the material world.

Prayer to Yogananda – *"My dear beloved Yogananda guruji, light up my darkness, awaken my soul, and help me find my inner peace so I may live in meaningful joy spreading happiness to my little world."*

You can connect with your chosen ascended masters in three simple ways: meditation and/or channeling your energy to receive their information. The process of meditation has already been discussed in the previous chapters. Here are a few simple steps on how you can use channeling to receive your master's words of wisdom:

1. Find an object through which you want to channel your energy. It could be your journal, Bible or book of your religion, canvas, or anything else you are attached to.
2. Find a quiet, undisturbed spot for the ritual.
3. Close your eyes and set the intention to call your master. Let the intention be simple but powerful. For example, *"I call upon Master Yogananda to come and sit with me now."*
4. Welcome your master and pose your question to him.
5. Use your chosen channel to write down the answers you hear or feel. Write what comes to mind. Remember, your master is speaking to you through your mind.
6. Initially, you may doubt the process. However, as you keep practicing it, you will notice hitherto hidden ideas and thoughts coming to the forefront, and answers are revealed to you.
7. Develop a strong bond with your ascended master to keep the communication strong between the two of you.

And finally, read up a lot about your chosen ascended master(s), learn from their life experiences, and implement what you learn into your life as much as you can. The more you try to mimic the life of your ascended master, the more your energy will align with their vibration. They will definitely respond to your call for help.

Chapter Nine: Working with Gods and Goddesses

This final chapter will focus on how to communicate with gods and goddesses who come as guardian angels to help you when you need to call upon them. Here, take a look at some of them with whom you may find a connection.

Find Your Guardian Angel from the Pantheon of Gods and Goddesses

Ganesha - The Hindu elephant god is known by many names, including Ganesha, Ganapati, Vignaharta, and others. He is the god of clearing obstacles. Hindus pray to him before starting any venture, seeking help to deal with potential obstacles in the endeavor. An annual festival in his honor is celebrated with great pomp all over India.

Ganesha, the god of clearing obstacles.
https://commons.wikimedia.org/wiki/File:Ganesha_Basohli_miniature_circa_1730_Dubost_p73.jpg

Seek his help to overcome all kinds of obstacles in your life. He may get rid of them or help you to overcome them. Call upon him, and he will come to your aid.

Prayer to Ganesha – *"Lord Ganesha, take care of the challenges in my path so I may succeed in my efforts. Give me the strength and courage to overcome struggles and come through unscathed and successfully."*

Devi - Devi is a powerful Hindu goddess, believed to be the female aspect of the creator and creation. She is the universal mother. Without her, the divine will would not have been able to create the world. Devi can appear as a nurturing, soft goddess or as an angry one who comes to destroy evil violently if needed.

In every village in India, she is worshiped in some form or other. She has a temple dedicated to her name in the village or town, and the people in that area consider her their family deity and pray to her for all their needs. She provides for them and protects her wards lovingly and unconditionally.

Pray to Devi for purifying your body and mind, getting rid of addictions, finding meaningfulness in your life, and for protection. Call upon her for all kinds of help, from materialistic needs to healing to spiritual uplifting. She will answer your call because she is the divine mother of all creation.

Prayer to Devi – *"Dear Goddess Devi, I pray to you for protection and comfort. Keep me safe from evil. Show me the path of love and help me deal with obstacles and challenges. Always be by my side. Teach me to discern between good and evil, so I may make the right choices."*

Kali – Kali is also a form of Devi. Kali means "black." Her black skin represents the darkness and evil that she has destroyed and consumed to protect her followers and believers. She destroys the strong bonds of materialism that bind people to their karmic wheel, and because of this, people are free to ascend into higher realms of consciousness.

Seek her help if you need to get rid of fear and uncertainties. She is the goddess of death when it comes to dealing with fear. Like a mother who keeps her children safe from danger, Ma Kali (Mother Kali) destroys evil and keeps you safe. Seek her help if you are struggling in the realms of determination, focus, motivation, direction, tenacity, and finding a guiding light in a dark world. She will illuminate your world for you.

Prayer to Goddess Kali – *"Dear Ma Kali, as you destroy the forces of evil for the good of humankind, destroy the negative bonds that bind me to the karmic wheel. Free me from this burden so I may find the path leading to you. Help me keep my levels of determination and focus high. Light up my darkness so I may remove fear from my body, mind, and soul."*

Diana – Diana is the goddess of the moon and of hunting. She stands for purity and is sought out by women who want to conceive. Women also seek her out for easy childbirth. Depicted as a tall and beautiful lady, she comes to the aid of all parents. Seek her help for matters regarding the breeding of animals, birthing and pregnancy, infertility issues, etc.

Prayer to Goddess Diana - *"Dear Goddess, keep my children safe from harm. Show me the path to being a healthy parent. Teach me what I need to know to raise my children well."*

Guinevere - Guinevere translates to "white shadow," and she is the Celtic goddess of motherhood, fertility, and love. She brings prosperity and fertility to the Earth. If you need to find your soulmate or true love, reach out to her for help. She helps to get rid of negative emotions like jealousy and desire for revenge. She deals with balance and harmony, ensuring you do not get stuck on the extreme ends of the spectrum.

Prayer to Guinevere (for conception) - *"Dear Goddess Guinevere, my husband and I want to have a child. Bless us so we can have one in your reflection. May he or she be conceived in my womb through your blessing. Grant me this boon."*

For finding your soulmate - *"Dear Goddess Guinevere, I'm lonely and lost in this racing world. Show me the path to my true love, the one who will stay with me (and I with him or her) until death do us part. Help me find my soulmate so we may build a new home together for our children."*

Krishna - Krishna was the reincarnation of Lord Vishnu, who took birth as a human to get rid of adharma (or injustice) and re-establish dharma (justice) on Earth. Every time the world overflows with adharma, Lord Vishnu takes birth (or a human avatar) to re-establish dharma. Krishna is Lord Vishnu's eighth avatar. He is depicted as a romantic, fun-loving person, although he can wield the gavel of justice uncompromisingly when the time comes. He renders joy and happiness to his bhaktas (or followers).

Pray to Lord Krishna for all things concerning romantic love, relationships and friendships, purification, protection, materialistic needs, spiritual awakening, and everything else in between. He is a bestower of blessings, and all he asks for is your unconditional love and surrender to him. He is known by thousands of names, including Krishna, Kanha, Balagopal, Gopal, Venugopal, and many more.

Prayer to Lord Krishna - *"Dear Krishna, you are the ultimate source of this cosmos. Without you, I am nothing. I surrender to you unconditionally. Show me the path I need to take and the work I need to* do. I will do your bidding and surrender the outcomes of my work to you."

Quan Yin - Quan Yin is the Chinese goddess of compassion, protection, and mercy. It is believed that this beautiful deity answers every prayer made to her, and she leaves no prayer unanswered. She loves humankind so much that even after enlightenment, she retained her human form rather than embracing Buddhahood.

In addition to compassion and mercy, she is the goddess of clairvoyance, beauty, musical abilities, femininity, and gentleness. She also teaches self-compassion and has an extra affinity for women and children. When you find yourself floundering in the midst of turmoil, seek her out for stability and groundedness.

Prayer to Quan Yin - *"Dear Goddess Quan Yin, bless me with your powerful compassion and mercy. Teach me to deal with my past mistakes with self-compassion and kindness. Protect my children and show me mercy if I have erred."*

Lakshmi - Lakshmi is the Hindu goddess of wealth and prosperity. Her primary role is to help humankind find income-generating careers to bring in wealth, an important element to human happiness. Seek her out for handsome rewards, especially in the form of material wealth and abundance.

If you find yourself stuck in a rut financially, Goddess Lakshmi is the one you should seek. She is the goddess of abundance, aesthetics, beauty, endurance, food, and balance between spirituality and materialism. She is depicted as a beautiful lady showering gold on her seekers.

Prayer to Goddess Lakshmi - *"Dear Goddess, bless me and my family with abundance. Remain in my home so we may never want for anything. Manifest my desires so my family and I can find the happiness we seek."*

Serapis Bey - Serapis Bey is the Egyptian god of the underworld. His primary role is to discipline people to begin the arduous journey toward ascension physically and spiritually. He motivates his followers to be physically fit and to adopt healthy lifestyles. Seek his help to deal with cravings and addictions, weight-loss and exercise-related stuff, fulfill prophecies, and ascend to higher planes of consciousness.

Prayer to Serapis Bey - *"Dear God of the Underworld, help me stay determined in my journey of physical fitness and healthy lifestyle. Bless* *me so I may avoid laziness and procrastination. Motivate me to achieve my best through hard work and determination. Protect me from the ills of cravings and undue desires."*

Hercules - The unparalleled hero of Roman-Greek legends, Hercules (Heracles in Greek) is not all masculine and show. He is a guardian angel, too, a warrior who loves humanity. He is known as the guardian of humankind, keeping you safe from perils and dangers. Pray to him for courage, strength, and tenacity.

Odin - Odin is the one-eyed All-Father in the Norse Pagan religion. He has numerous powers and responsibilities assigned to him. His speed and strength are unmatched, and he is also known to control space and time. Seek his help if you want to develop your mental, emotional, and physical strength.

Thor - Thor is the Norse god of thunder. He is the son of Odin, another important deity in Scandinavian mythology. Thor can fight evil spirits, negativity, and even dragons to keep his wards, including men and gods, safe and protected.

Frigga - Frigga is the wife of Odin. She has the power of foresight and also the ability to change the course of destiny. Seek her help when you feel stuck in a rut and want positive changes in your life.

How to Connect with Gods and Goddesses

There are many ways to connect with gods and goddesses, and they are discussed here, starting with the easiest and the most effective way, namely through prayer.

Prayers - Praying to your chosen deity is nothing more complex than talking to him or her. You can pray using scripted prayers or create your own, such as the ones given in the chapter for some of the gods. Praying can be a formal affair, where you sit in front of an altar and follow certain rituals, or informal, where you just sit quietly and speak to your god. Prayers form the foundation of any spiritual practice. Include prayers in your daily routine and embrace the happiness and purpose that seeps into your life from the divine plane.

Meditation - Like all forms of meditation, sit quietly and comfortably in a spot where you will not be disturbed, close your eyes, and meditate on the form of your chosen deity. You can also use a mantra to repeat during the meditation session. This mantra could be a positive affirmation toward a specific purpose or a chant that hails your deity, seeking his or her blessings.

Read - You can read from your favorite holy book to connect with your god. As a Christian, read your favorite passages from the Bible. Take a shloka from the Bhagavad Gita and read it like a mantra. Take a verse from the Koran and read it. Whatever religion you follow, read sacred books of that religion, and you will find yourself getting increasingly closer to your chosen deities. Every poem, hymn, song, verse, or chant which includes God's names can be used for this purpose. Include spiritual reading into your daily prayer routine.

The more seasoned spiritual people use advanced methods of communicating with gods and goddesses. They use journeying into the other worlds or altering their consciousness so that they can be led to the other-worlds to communicate with their chosen deity. For beginners and novices, the three methods mentioned above, particularly prayers, work wonders.

The more you practice communicating with your deities, the stronger your bond will become. Your ability to hear their messages and interpret the signs and signals they send you will improve. Talking to your guardian angels will soon become like talking to your best friend on planet Earth.

Conclusion

To summarize, guardian angels are spiritual beings living in the spiritual realm but with the hope, intention, and God-given role of being humankind's assistants. Archangels are created by God Himself to follow His commands and to help humankind. Every archangel has a specific role to play, although you can reach out to any of them for all kinds of help. The other kinds of spirit guides and guardian angels already want to help you in their own ways; you just need to reach out to them.

Guardian angels and spirit guides can appear in any form and speak to you in a variety of ways. Animal guides come in the form of animals (as the name suggests), and ancestor spirits come to take your offerings and help you deal with family issues. All of this may seem a bit weird at the beginning of your practice, especially since you are still stuck in the five-sensory limited world.

The trick to overcoming the physical world's limitations is to open your heart and mind. The problem with most people is that they are scared to open their hearts for various reasons. Most importantly, the fear of the unknown and the fear of the pain of losing what they already have. Further, people tend to carry their past pain into the future and are scared to be hurt again. And so, they close their hearts and live within the apparent security that "limitations" give them.

You need to find the strength to break these limiting barriers and experience all that you deserve in the physical world and the realms beyond. And for that, you have to open your hearts. Here are a few tips

to that end before we end this book:
- **Accept your pain**. *Pain never kills;* it only makes you focus on it so you can find the root of the problem and solve it. Dealing with pain sensibly makes you stronger and better than before.
- **Move out of your comfort zone**. The more you stay in the ease of your comfort zone, the more rigid and inflexible your heart and mind will become. Keep moving out of your comfort zone to build resistance and resilience.
- **Speak to your heart and ask what it wants**. Deal with its fears and show that you care. Your heart will respond in the same way.
- **Identify, engage with, and embrace your dark side as well**. No one is perfect. All people are flawed, and their strengths and weaknesses make each person unique. Accepting your weaknesses is the first step to acknowledging your authenticity. It is easy to accept your strengths. But it is equally important to identify and accept your dark side as well for a wholesome life experience. Your heart will thank you for it and open itself up for new experiences, a key element to going beyond the physical world.

Spend time alone and spend time with others in equal and balanced measures. First, spend time alone to understand yourself and know your uniqueness. What defines you? What gives you joy? What makes you sad? Once you know yourself, then go out into the world and be with people so you can learn from them and complement the gaps in your life in different ways. Engaging with the outside world also allows you to know that the strengths you have taken for granted are gaping holes in the lives of others. Slowly but surely, you'll learn about the wondrous interconnectedness of the universe, and your heart will open wide to accept all things that come in the future.

Engaging with spiritual beings starts from within and ends in a place that brings the entire cosmos to your heart. So, go on, start the wondrous journey toward your guardian angels with an open heart, and your mind and soul will follow.

Here's another book by Mari Silva that you might like

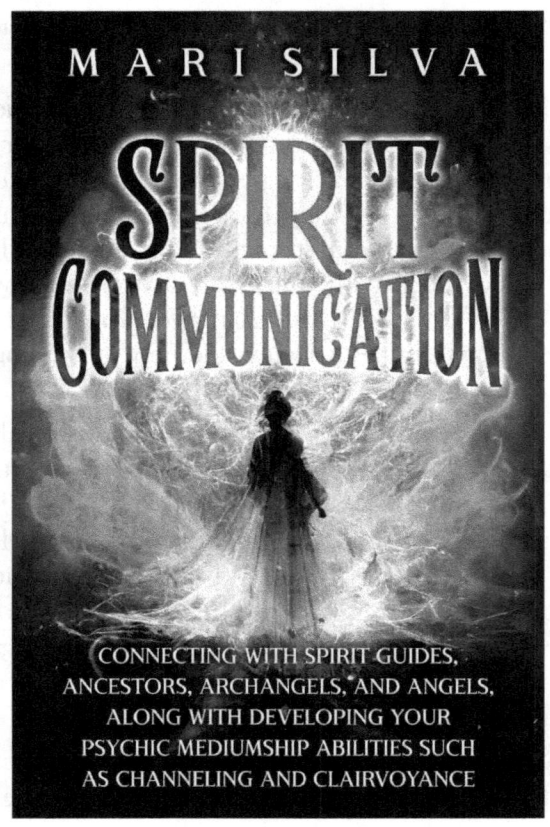

Your Free Gift
(only available for a limited time)

Thanks for getting this book! If you want to learn more about various spirituality topics, then join Mari Silva's community and get a free guided meditation MP3 for awakening your third eye. This guided meditation mp3 is designed to open and strengthen ones third eye so you can experience a higher state of consciousness. Simply visit the link below the image to get started.

https://spiritualityspot.com/meditation

References

"5 Powerful Signs of Archangel Gabriel Reaching out to You." Www.alittlesparkofjoy.com, 18 Aug. 2021, https://www.alittlesparkofjoy.com/archangel-gabriel/

"5 Tips for Creating a Sacred Space." HuffPost, 19 Apr. 2013, www.huffpost.com/entry/sacred-space_b_3094267.

"6 Types of Spirit Guides & How to Communicate with Them." Mindbodygreen, 23 Jan. 2015, www.mindbodygreen.com/articles/types-of-spirit-guides.

"7 Healing Angels to Call upon for Your Chakras." Soul and Spirit, 18 May 2017, www.soulandspiritmagazine.com/7-angels-call-upon-chakras/.

"7 Shocking Ways Angels Speak to You Every Day." Psych Central, 24 July 2016, https://psychcentral.com/blog/life-goals/2016/07/ways-angels-speak-to-you#2.-Feelings-and-Physical-Sensations-.

"7 Shocking Ways Angels Speak to You Every Day." Psych Central, 24 July 2016, https://psychcentral.com/blog/life-goals/2016/07/ways-angels-speak-to-you#6.-Signs-and-Symbols.

"7 Signs Your Guardian Angel Is Trying to Contact You – Buddha & Karma." Buddhaandkarma.com, https://buddhaandkarma.com/blogs/guide/signs-your-guardian-angel-is-trying-to-contact-you

"10 "Higher Self" Journal Prompts." A Great Mood, 17 Oct. 2022, https://agreatmood.com/higher-self-journal-prompts/#.

"11 Feather Color Meanings: The Significance of Feathers and What They Symbolize." Color Meanings, 22 Aug. 2020, www.color-meanings.com/feather-color-meanings-symbolism/.

"12 Archangels: Their Names, Meanings, Traits, and Their Connection with Zodiac Signs and Birth Dates." WILLOW SOUL, https://willowsoul.com/blogs/angels/12-archangels-names-meanings-traits-zodiac-signs-birth-date

"12 Signs an Angel Messenger Is near - Centre of Excellence." Www.centreofexcellence.com, www.centreofexcellence.com/angel-messenger-12-signs/#.

"A Quick Guide to Chakra Meditation | BetterSleep." Www.bettersleep.com, www.bettersleep.com/blog/a-quick-guide-to-chakra-meditation/.

admin. "The Seven Angels of the Week ★ Angelorum." Angelorum, 16 Dec. 2014, https://angelorum.co/topics/angels/the-seven-angels-of-the-week/

Aletheia. "7 Ways to Connect with Your Spirit Animal." LonerWolf, 6 Feb. 2014, https://lonerwolf.com/spirit-animal/#h-7-ways-to-discover-your-spirit-animal.

Anthony, Kym. "Our 6 Favourite Crystals for Awakening Your Spiritual Self-Awareness!" Luna Tide, 20 Oct. 2021, https://luna-tide.com/blogs/journal/crystals-for-awakening.

"Archangel & Zodiac Signs | a Spiritual Connection - AstroTalk.com." AstroTalk Blog - Online Astrology Consultation with Astrologer, 3 Mar. 2020, https://astrotalk.com/astrology-blog/archangel-and-zodiac-signs/.

"ARCHANGEL GABRIEL and CANCER." Tumblr, www.tumblr.com/whoismyguardianangel/148402320155/archangel-gabriel-and-cancer.

"ARCHANGEL JEREMIEL and SCORPIO." Tumblr, www.tumblr.com/whoismyguardianangel/148402117040/archangel-jeremiel-and-scorpio.

"ARCHANGEL ZADKIEL and GEMINI." Tumblr, www.tumblr.com/whoismyguardianangel/148402350110/archangel-zadkiel-and-gemini.

"Are Auras Real? 16 FAQs about Color, Meaning, More." Healthline, 5 Jan. 2022, www.healthline.com/health/what-is-an-aura#presence-of-colors.

B. A., English. "Acknowledging Guardian Angels in Islam." Learn Religions, www.learnreligions.com/muslim-guardian-angel-prayers-124056.

---. "How Archangels Can Help You Balance Your Life." Learn Religions, www.learnreligions.com/archangels-of-four-directions-124410.

---. "How to Know When Archangel Zadkiel Is Near." Learn Religions, www.learnreligions.com/how-to-recognize-archangel-zadkiel-124287.

---. "How to Recognize Archangel Raziel." Learn Religions, www.learnreligions.com/how-to-recognize-archangel-raziel-124282.

Beckett, John. "6 Ways to Talk to the Gods (and How to Listen for an Answer)." John Beckett, 4 Oct. 2018, www.patheos.com/blogs/johnbeckett/2018/10/6-ways-to-talk-to-the-gods.html.

Benner, Mara. "Learn 5 Ways to Connect with Your Loved Ones in Spirit -." Four Directions Wellness, 27 Oct. 2019, https://fourdirectionswellness.com/2019/10/27/learn-5-ways-to-connect-with-your-loved-ones-in-spirit/

"Higher Self: 3 Effective Ways to Connect to the Guidance Within." Soul Scroll Journals, https://soulscrolljournals.com/blogs/news/higher-self-3-effective-ways-to-connect-to-the-guidance-within

"How Does a Guardian Angel Work?" Catholic Answers, www.catholic.com/magazine/online-edition/how-does-a-guardian-angel-work.

"How to Get to Know Your Guardian Angels + Unlock Their Power." Mindbodygreen, 24 May 2016, www.mindbodygreen.com/articles/how-to-get-to-know-your-guardian-angels.

"How to Recognize Archangel Chamuel." Learn Religions, www.learnreligions.com/how-to-recognize-archangel-chamuel-124273.

"How to Recognize Archangel Michael." Learn Religions, www.learnreligions.com/how-to-recognize-archangel-michael-124278.

"How to Recognize Ariel, Angel of Nature." Learn Religions, www.learnreligions.com/how-to-recognize-archangel-ariel-124271.

"How Your Guardian Angel May Send You Messages through Scents." Learn Religions, www.learnreligions.com/contacting-your-angel-scent-messages-124357.

"LEO and ARCHANGEL RAZIEL." Tumblr, www.tumblr.com/whoismyguardianangel/148402290140/leo-and-archangel-raziel.

McGinley, Karson. "7 Chakra Meditations to Keep You in Balance." Chopra, 3 Feb. 2020, https://chopra.com/articles/7-chakra-meditations-to-keep-you-in-balance

"Meet Archangel Jophiel, Angel of Beauty." Learn Religions, www.learnreligions.com/meet-archangel-jophiel-124094.

Nast, Condé. "Everything You Need to Know about Angel Numbers." Allure, 24 Dec. 2021, www.allure.com/story/what-are-angel-numbers.

Oinam, Goutamkumar. "Mythology about Guardian Gods across the World." Medium, 17 Feb. 2022, medium.com/@goutamkumaroina/mythology-about-guardian-gods-across-the-world-7cf662780198.

"Rapheael, Michael, Gabriel, Uriel: Archangels of the 4 Nature Elements." Learn Religions, www.learnreligions.com/archangels-of-four-elements-in-nature-124411.

Shah, Parita. "The Chopra Center." The Chopra Center, 14 May 2019, https://chopra.com/articles/what-is-a-chakra

Silva, Jorge. "9 Cloud Symbolism & Spiritual Meanings (and Dark Cloud." Angelical Balance, 3 Sept. 2022, www.angelicalbalance.com/spirituality/cloud-symbolism-spiritual-meaning/#9_Cloud_Symbolism_and_Spiritual_Meanings.

"Sugilite Meaning- Physical, Mental, & Spiritual Healing Properties." Tiny Rituals, https://tinyrituals.co/blogs/tiny-rituals/sugilite-meaning

"The Ascended Masters: Who Are They and How Can They Help?" Kaliana Emotional Care, www.kaliana.com/blogs/eatdrinkthink/the-ascended-masters-who-they-are-and-how-they-can-help.

"The Four Bodies - Physical, Emotional, Mental & Spiritual." Goop, 9 Apr. 2015, https://goop.com/wellness/spirituality/the-four-bodies/

The Four Important Archangels. www.divineblessingsforall.com/the-four-important-archangels/.

The Seven Chakras – Vortexes of Power. www.himalayanyogainstitute.com/the-seven-chakras-vortexes-of-power/.

Tran, Dung. "Angel Meditation for Keeping in Touch with Your Angels." Medium, 2 July 2018, medium.com/@dunglongtran/angel-meditation-for-keeping-in-touch-with-your-angels-df2a3b6961d2.

Vaudoise, Mallorie. "A Ritual to Reconnect with Your Ancestors." Spirituality & Health, 24 Nov. 2019, www.spiritualityhealth.com/articles/2019/11/24/a-ritual-to-reconnect-with-your-ancestors.

"Visualizing Your Guardian Angel." Www.beliefnet.com, www.beliefnet.com/faiths/faith-tools/meditation/2007/03/visualizing-your-guardian-angel.aspx.

"Who Is Archangel Michael & 5 Sings of the Great Protector." Www.alittlesparkofjoy.com, 10 May 2021, https://www.alittlesparkofjoy.com/archangel-michael/

"Who Your Guardian Angel Is and What They Do: 10 Things." Holyart.com Blog, 16 May 2018, www.holyart.com/blog/religious-items/who-your-guardian-angel-is-and-what-they-do-10-things-you-should-know/.

Wong, Kenneth. "The 7 Archangels: Names, Meanings and Duties." The Millennial Grind, 5 July 2021, https://millennial-grind.com/the-7-archangels-and-their-roles/

"Yoga and Consciousness: A Meditation to Access Your Highest Self." Healthline, 15 Nov. 2021, www.healthline.com/health/fitness/yoga-and-consciousness#A-meditation-for-consciousness.

Yugay, Irina. "How to Connect with Your Higher Self, according to Spirituality Teachers." Mindvalley Blog, 10 May 2022, https://blog.mindvalley.com/higher-self/

www.ingramcontent.com/pod-product-compliance
Lightning Source LLC
Chambersburg PA
CBHW072152200426
43209CB00052B/1147